ARIS & PHILLIPS HISPANIC CLASSICS

MIGUEL DE UNAMUNO

An Anthology of his Poetry

Translation, Introduction and Notes by

C. A. Longhurst

Aris & Phillips is an imprint of Oxbow Books

Published in the United Kingdom in 2015 by
OXBOW BOOKS
10 Hythe Bridge Street, Oxford OX1 2EW

and in the United States by
OXBOW BOOKS
908 Darby Road, Havertown, PA 19083

Original Spanish poems © heirs of Miguel de Unamuno
Translation © C. A. Longhurst 2015

Hardback Edition: ISBN 978-1-91057-227-6
Paperback Edition: ISBN 978-1-91057-218-4
Digital Edition: ISBN 978-1-91057-219-1

A CIP record for this book is available from the British Library

For a complete list of Aris & Phillips titles, please contact:

UNITED KINGDOM	UNITED STATES OF AMERICA
Oxbow Books	Oxbow Books
Telephone (01865) 241249	Telephone (800) 791-9354
Fax (01865) 794449	Fax (610) 853-9146
Email: oxbow@oxbowbooks.com	Email: queries@casemateacademic.com
www.oxbowbooks.com	www.casemateacademic.com/oxbow

Oxbow Books is part of the Casemate group

Front cover: Parc Guell by Gaudi tile

Printed and bound by CPI Group (UK) Ltd, Croydon, CR0 4YY

To the memory of Gareth Alban Davies
poet, scholar, and friend

CONTENTS

IV   Exile

V   Language and Poetry

VI   Philosophical Meditations

Conclusion

INTRODUCTION

Unamuno's Poetic Production

This bilingual anthology is intended to introduce the poetry of Miguel de Unamuno to English readers unfamiliar with it, and also to readers who have an interest in translation from Spanish into English. At the same time it offers a way of approaching Unamuno that differs from a reading of his novels, plays, and essays. The poetry conveys a somewhat different impression of Unamuno the man and the writer: more sensitive, mindful, and restrained; less impetuous, vehement, and defiant.

The selection represents but a tiny proportion of the poetic output of Unamuno, one of the most prolific poets in the whole of Spanish literature. The fifty poems presented here amount to just two percent of his production of approximately 2,500 poems. I hope all the same that it offers a taster of this unjustly neglected poet. I say unjustly neglected not because he has been totally neglected in the Spanish-speaking world, but rather because as a poet Unamuno has not had the attention he merits in comparison with either Spanish poets of his own time (those who wrote between 1900 and 1936) or his own non-poetic production, and particularly his prose fiction. He is, for example, close in style and spirit to Antonio Machado (who thought highly of Unamuno and was influenced by him), yet Machado's poetry has enjoyed far more scholarly and critical attention than Unamuno's. Juan Ramón Jiménez, widely perceived as the other great Spanish poet of the time alongside Antonio Machado, also recognized Unamuno's stature as a poet, despite the fact that he was very different from himself; and the great Nicaraguan poet Rubén Darío, whose poetry did not appeal to Unamuno, wrote that even within the traditional forms that Unamuno preferred, his poetry reached unexpected lyrical depths. Unusually, Unamuno's poetry has been better received among poets than among critics, and to those mentioned could be added the names of Luis Felipe Vivanco and Luis Cernuda. Part of the critical neglect of Unamuno's poetry is due to the simple fact that his novels and quasi-philosophical essays have been perceived as more innovative, and have therefore attracted more critical interest. Yet Unamuno himself prized his poetry above his novels, plays, and essays, and it was as a poet that he longed to be remembered. An anecdote has survived that tells of an interviewer saying to Unamuno: 'Sé que usted hace también poesías' ['I know you also compose poetry']. To which Unamuno replied: 'No. Lo que hago también son las otras cosas' ['No. What I also compose is the other stuff']. Time and again he claimed that it was in the poems that his authentic voice could be found: 'Lo que hago con más gusto es la poesía' ['What I take most pleasure in writing is poetry'].

Unamuno started publishing poetry comparatively late in life. We know he wrote occasional poems in the 1890s, when he was in his thirties, but his first collection of poems was not published until 1907 in his native city of Bilbao, when Unamuno was nearly 43, and was titled simply *Poesías*. It contained 102 poems of very diverse form and content divided into sixteen sections according to subject and including five verse translations or reconstructions from four of Unamuno's favourite poets, Coleridge, Leopardi, Carducci, and his almost exact contemporary Maragall. Home life, the land, the search for transcendent values are topics with a strong presence. In this first collection blank verse predominates over rhyme; indeed Unamuno originally despised rhyme because he thought it enslaved thought, forcing it to choose unwanted words. But he was soon to change his mind and eventually declared that rhyme was in fact a source of creativity. This first book of poetry attracted little attention, but Rubén Darío, already famous by then, wrote a highly sympathetic review eighteen months later. (Poems Nos 1, 4, 6, 7, 10, 16, 17, in this anthology, come from this collection.)

The second collection of poems was *Rosario de sonetos líricos* (1911), which, surprisingly, builds on a short section in the preceding collection which had used the sonnet form. Whereas the earlier poetry revealed a preference for the Romantics (especially English and Italian), with the expression of strong sentiments but with inadequate control over metre, in *Rosario* Unamuno limits himself to the traditional sonnet form (probably the strictest verse form in Spanish), reminiscent of Quevedo, which imposes greater discipline and which he uses to good effect. With some exceptions, the 127 poems in this collection are, however, less personal and spontaneous and rather more literary, with citations from great writers and religious personalities, but this in itself serves as an indication that Unamuno always saw his work as a dialogue with writers who had preceded him. (Nos 3, 14, 15, 19, 25, 39 come from this collection.)

Unamuno's most famous poetic composition, *El Cristo de Velázquez*, followed in 1920. It is a vast composition, consisting of over 2,500 hendecasyllabic blank verses in four parts with a total of 89 separate poems or sections of varying length. It took many years to compose and is regarded in Spain as one of Unamuno's greatest works, indeed the only poetic work of his that is consistently mentioned. It was written, according to Unamuno himself, as self-imposed penance for an earlier poem on the wooden statue of Christ found in the Convent of St Clare in Palencia, in which the recumbent and heavily bloodstained figure is described in brutal and dismissive terms in what is a clear denunciation of the bleak traditional Christianity of Castile focussed on a dead Jesus.[1] Regarded in Spain as one of the greatest religious poems in the Spanish language, the 'Christ of Velázquez' poem elaborates on features of the seventeenth-century painter's portrait of Christ crucified, with accompanying meditations on Christ's role in our lives, but despite some moving passages and an extraordinary array of biblical allusions Unamuno's Christology is opaque.[2] The poem seems to be mainly a tribute to the suffering Christ, the suffering not of a god but of a human being. Rather than theology it offers human compassion and empathy. The panegyrical comments of some Spanish commentators are a little hard to accept if one does not share the Spanish predilection for crucifixion iconography. The poem is certainly impressive, but perhaps more for its descriptive power or ecphrasis and for the labour that has gone into it than for its ability to move us to a genuine spiritual experience, with the possible exception of the impassioned final plea for salvation from death of the closing section; in any case its length virtually precludes reading and absorbing it at one sitting.[3]

Andanzas y visiones españolas (1922) was in the main a prose work which contained a dozen poems composed some time earlier, but of which some were now rendered in continuous prose rather than verse,

---

1   This devotion to the dead Jesus, as distinct from the resurrected Jesus, was denounced by many liberal Spanish writers of the time, *e.g.* Clarín, Baroja, Gabriel Miró.

2   For a lucid commentary on this aspect, see Eamonn Rodgers, 'The Christ of Velázquez and the Christ of Unamuno', *Bulletin of Spanish Studies*, XCII:1 (2015), 51–63.

3   *El Cristo de Velázquez* is available in both English and French translations: Miguel de Unamuno, *The Velázquez Christ*, translated by William Thomas Little (Lanham, MD: University Press of America, 2002); Pilar de Cuadra, *Étude sur le Poème de Miguel de Unamuno 'Le Christ de Velazquez'*, *avec une traduction intégrale* (Paris: Institut Catholique de Paris, 1987).

according to Unamuno in order to avoid giving the potential buyer of
the book the impression that he was getting a lot of blank space for his
money. Like the rest of the book, the poems are concerned with various
locations and landscapes and include one on Salamanca and another
on Bilbao (the two places closest to Unamuno's heart), together with
the notorious poem 'The Recumbent Christ of Santa Clara at Palencia'
mentioned above, but here presented in continuous prose. Rather more
important poetically is *Rimas de dentro* (1923), a limited first edition
which circulated privately. It was a small collection of twenty poems on
a variety of themes similar to those found in the first collection, *Poesías*,
such as domestic life, places and landscapes, and some philosophical
meditations. (Nos 41 and 42 in this anthology.) One interesting feature
of *Rimas de dentro* is that in several of the poems – and as the title of the
collection implies – there is a complex internal rhyming scheme, which
betrays an interest, perhaps temporary, in more experimental forms of
verse.

   Teresa. Rimas de un poeta desconocido (1924) followed a year later.
Here Unamuno poses as editor rather than author (as Antonio Machado
did with his fictitious poet-philosopher Abel Martín). This allegedly
posthumous collection is made up of ninety-nine poems which Rafael,
the 'author' of the poems, had dedicated to his dead fiancée, Teresa,
before sending them to Unamuno for approval. We can take this to be
a more or less entertaining gimmick recalling Cervantes's Cide Hamete
Benengeli or so many other literary alter egos, or we may opt to see
it as an unfolding of the self – a typically Unamunian strategy used in
several of his novels – in which creator and creature establish a dialogue
of mutual discovery (Unamuno's view of God was altogether similar, a
process of mutual creation). The overwhelming subject of the collection
is love, and commentators have seen the footprint of the mid-nineteenth-
century Spanish poet Gustavo Adolfo Bécquer in these poems (following
Unamuno's own indication of influences). Some poems clearly do echo
this late Romantic Spanish poet;[4] yet at the same time this new twentieth-
century Bécquer adds a sense of tragic irony to the old. One wonders,
too, whether Unamuno's vision of love is really Bécquer's. There is
something entirely metaphysical often mixed up with the love theme, the

---

4   For example 'Eres tú mi poesía' based on Bécquer's 'poesía eres tú' in poem No. 21
of his *Libro de los gorriones*.

desire to reach out to some transcendent dimension of existence. There is considerable metric variety, with either assonance or strong rhyme.

De Fuerteventura a París (1925), another collection of sonnets, was published in Paris while Unamuno was living there after his return to Europe in July 1924 after a four-month exile on the island. Of the 103 poems in this collection sixty-four were written on the island, a couple on board ship on the way to Cherbourg, and the remainder in Paris. Although there are many fine poems here, some describing the barren land of Fuerteventura and many more the seas around it, usually with a symbolic intention, the collection as a whole is vitiated by Unamuno's repeated invective against the Spanish authorities in Madrid responsible for his exile. While Unamuno's indignation is wholly justified, his bitter, often ironic, denunciations of the regime in Spain do nothing for the poetic quality of the verse. Enough remains, however, worthy of anthologising, and four poems are included here (Nos 26, 27, 28, 29). Also from his years of exile is *Romancero del destierro* (1928), published in Buenos Aires, which collects fifty-five poems written during his first two years of exile in Hendaye (he arrived there from Paris in August 1925). Although his attacks on the Spanish government and the Spanish monarch continued and gained a good deal in ironic disdain, the long period of retreat in Hendaye from 1925 to early 1930 were on the whole peaceful and poetically fruitful years for Unamuno, years of reading, writing, and quiet meditation. Despite suffering the discomforts of exile and of living away from home he felt relatively at ease in the familiar surroundings of his youth, the Basque Country, in this case of course the Pyrénées Atlantiques of South West France. Of the fifty-five poems in this collection, eighteen adopt the popular and traditional octosyllabic verse form of the *romance* or ballad, but it is largely an ironic use of the form because most of these are in fact poems of political protest, not of heroic deeds in battle as in the medieval ballads of war between Christians and Moors. The rest of the collection is typically diverse within the parameters of Unamuno's preoccupations, and four are included here (Nos 32, 33, 45, 47).

The *Cancionero*, first published in Buenos Aires in 1953 by the distinguished pupil of Unamuno Federico de Onís, collects Unamuno's poetic production from 1928 until his death on the last day of 1936. It also has an introduction by Unamuno himself which provides some insight into his approach to poetry. With 1,755 poems (some critics argue the real number should be nearer 1,800), the *Cancionero* is such a vast compendium as to defy all generalization. Its very diversity in subject-matter and poetic form serves rather to emphasize Unamuno's extraordinary versatility as a writer. There is probably a simplification of expression compared to his early poetry, but on the other hand there is a much more pronounced use of conceit in the style of Quevedo. The use of paradox, riddles, etymologies, and punning makes it a rich but discontinuous book of poetry, a book which impresses by its sheer prolixity, with here and there half-a-dozen or even a dozen poems bearing the same date, an indication perhaps of a sustained attempt to combat intellectual boredom during his later years in Hendaye. Many of those written after May 1934 are devoted to the memory of Concha, his wife. The originality of this vast collection is unquestionable, but it is originality of a rather bewildering sort. A sensitive selection would have done wonders for the public perception of the quality of the *Cancionero*, but Unamuno steadfastly refused to reject any of his 'children' as he called his poems (see for example No. 41). Of course the collection itself is posthumous and Unamuno had no direct hand in finally putting it together, although he had planned it. Twenty-two of the fifty poems in this anthology (Nos 5, 8, 9, 11, 12, 13, 18, 20, 21, 22, 30, 31, 34, 35, 36, 37, 38, 40, 43, 44, 46, 50), spread over all six sections, come from the *Cancionero*. Many of the poems in the *Cancionero* have to do with language and the function of writing (one poem being devoted to the linguistician Fritz Mauthner), suggesting that Unamuno's preoccupation with language had intensified in later life.

In addition to these various collections of poems, other poems that were found not to have been included in any of them were published in 1958 as *Poesías sueltas*, subsequently enlarged as more poems were located, now amounting to 114 poems, but it is highly likely that there are still poems lying forgotten in newspapers and magazines of Unamuno's day. Five poems from *Poesías sueltas* are included here (Nos 2, 23, 24, 48, 49).

Poetic Themes

I said earlier that Unamuno's poetic production evinces a great diversity of subject-matter. It is equally true, however, that there are certain recurrent preoccupations, just as there are in Unamuno's work as a whole. These preoccupations or themes, or at least some of them, are reflected in the sections chosen for this anthology. The major evolution in Unamuno's thought takes place in the years around or immediately before 1900 (from a positivistic stance in his earliest works towards the adoption of a much more spiritual outlook thereafter), and therefore this change does not affect his poetry, virtually all of which was written after 1900. There is some evolution in his use of poetic forms, from a freer, less disciplined verse towards a greater use of well established forms, but the change is not so distinct as to radically affect his production. I have therefore chosen not to arrange the poems in this anthology chronologically, preferring instead a thematic arrangement in six sections. Though in no way watertight – Unamuno often mixes different sentiments and ideas in the same poem – these thematic sections help to give a better idea of his range. Let us look at some of these themes in a little more detail to extract some essential aspects of Unamuno's thought as revealed in his poetry.

Home Life

The significance of the family is a topic that appears in virtually all of Unamuno's work. Love between spouses and interdependence of parents and children are also emphasized in many novels and possibly reflects in some way Unamuno's own personal experience in the way he was brought up by his mother and grandmother after the early loss of his father. He wrote many poems, among the most beautiful of his entire production, devoted to the impact which his wife, Concha Lizárraga, had on him, and also poems about his children or children in general, and these poems need little comment. They variously express affection, concern (especially of course those referring to his hydrocephalic son, Raimundín), surprise, delight and occasionally puzzlement at a child's view of the world. Poem No. 7, for instance, shows a child at play imaginatively infusing life into his rough drawing of a doll. The poems about family and home life provide a glimpse into the more private side of Unamuno. Here we observe the peaceful family man for whom home is a sacred place that offers security and a sense of continuity (*e.g.* poems No. 1, No. 2). The tone of these poems is more restrained than many dealing with human fate or national conflict.

At the centre of the family lies Concha, whose presence is reassuring and consoling. Serene, constant, quietly confident in her religious faith,

Concha played a comparable role in life and in poetry. In life she helped Unamuno recover from a life-threatening attack of depression in the late 1890s, and throughout her married life she provided a solid, dependable environment for the volatile Miguel. There is even a poem (not included in this anthology) in which Unamuno expresses a sense of shame at his own despondency in the face of Concha's joyful radiance. Since Unamuno was subject to bouts of dysthymia, there is little doubt that Concha exercised a saving influence, and indeed in poem No. 2 she is portrayed as his saviour. In another poem (not included here) he refers to her as 'mi ancla, mi costumbre' ['my anchor, my habit']. In poem No. 3 she is seen as the solver of the Delphic riddles, of life's enigmas; in her imperturbability she seems to know the secret of eternity, an aspect that Unamuno also recalls in what is perhaps the most beautiful poem of all those he wrote as a tribute after her death (No. 5); and in poem No. 8 we can sense the enormous void that her disappearance has left in Unamuno as he struggles to affirm her continuing presence: Concha has dominated his life, and continues to do so after her death. In all, his wife and family inspired some of Unamuno's most appealing and heartfelt poetry. Not only that, but it is love of the family that is the ultimate tamer of his rebellious nature in the face of both earthly and celestial conflict. It is above all the example of Concha and her confident and amiable outlook that reconciled him in his final years to the fact of death, to death as a door opening onto a new life, as is detectable in some of his late poems (*e.g.* No. 11).

The one thing we do notice about poems 1, 2, 3, and 6 is that the presence of the family in no way removes the preoccupation with mortality, but rather serves to put it in a special light: somehow the love that unites Unamuno to his family appears, unlike the human person, to be indestructible. Of course this is not something that we find just in Unamuno (including, though in a more abstract way, his philosophical essay *Del sentimiento trágico de la vida en los hombres y en los pueblos* [*The Tragic Sense of Life in Men and in Peoples*]); it is found in all Christian existentialists, notably so in Gabriel Marcel and Nikolai Berdyaev, who see selfless human love in its other-directedness as a pointer to divine transcendence. For Unamuno clearly the family is the main focus of inter-subjective relatedness, but it is not limited to the immediate family; indeed one could say that family in Unamuno really stands for community. This idea of community as a way of transcending our material circumstances and limitations, so central to novels such as *La tía Tula*[5] and *San Manuel Bueno, mártir*, appears more implicitly in many poems not directly concerned with the immediate family circle but with the wider community of friends, of hard-working folk, and even of the departed (as in poem No. 11 or No. 32). A sense of communion is one of the key constituents in Unamuno's writing in general and the poetry in particular. And communion for Unamuno meant communion not just with his own private circle of family and friends but with his readers too (as we observe in poem No. 10).

The Land

In the poems that deal with the land Unamuno habitually brings in the local inhabitants, and it is their stoicism and uncomplaining nature in the face of hardship that he tends to single out. In poem No. 29 he refers to his experience of the island of Fuerteventura as a spiritual oasis, and in another dedicated to the island ('Oh, fuerteventurosa isla africana' ['Oh, venturesome African isle'], not included in this anthology) he speaks of the 'tesoro de salud y de nobleza' ['treasure of health and nobility'] that characterizes this dry, sparsely populated island, and of the 'limpio caudal de tu pobreza' ['untarnished wealth of your poverty']. He is of course exalting the spirit of the *majoreros*, the native people of the island, who led impoverished lives yet received their visitor warmly and generously. In poem No. 28 he contrasts the poverty of the land with the spiritual outlook of the inhabitants of Fuerteventura. This for Unamuno represents the spirit of genuine communality that could rescue peninsular Spain from its fractious and conflictive existence. We observe a similar sentiment of solidarity in 'The Voice of the Bell' (poem No. 23), in which Unamuno compares the life of the countryfolk of western Castile to the chimes of bells in the silence of a dawn, pure song without words. The people bear no grudge, they voice no complaint, they ask no favours. They simply dream of a better life when the harshness of this one is over. A similar sentiment of solidarity with the toilers on a stony soil is found in 'Reminiscence' (poem No. 49), an impressive invocation of the stoicism of the peasants of Castile.

---

5 Available in an English translation by Julia Biggane, *Aunt Tula*, in the Aris and Phillips Hispanic Classics series.

In a descriptive essay entitled 'Paisajes del alma' ['Landscapes of the Soul'], later used as title for an entire collection of such essays, Unamuno compares the view of the mountain from the plain with the view of the plain from the mountain. It quickly becomes apparent as we read that Unamuno is not simply describing the physical landscape. The landscape is a metaphor of the conflicting tendencies within man, the heights and the plains, the spiritual and the material, as they contemplate each other enviously yet longingly. This tendency to use the earth and the sky metaphorically permeates Unamuno's descriptive poems. It does not replace the description of physical traits but rather adds a metaphysical dimension to it. The Castilian landscape becomes a mirror of the human soul struggling to combat its state of barrenness, to achieve plenitude. Looking up towards the Gredos range becomes a symbol of spiritual aspiration, and observing the rainfall a symbol of promise of future fulfilment. In this respect Unamuno is harking back to another Salamanca poet, the sixteenth-century Augustinian friar Luis de León, who also used nature metaphorically (and to whom Unamuno often alluded admiringly).

There is therefore in Unamuno a close connection between the surrounding natural world – old towns, the countryside, the sea – and the spiritual world. The barrenness of the island of Fuerteventura, its material poverty, is compensated by a spiritual richness suggested by the mysterious, heaving seas around it. We never find those exotic gardens of *modernista* poetry in the style of Rubén Darío; Unamuno's landscapes are nearly always harsh, bare, rocky, as is of course the real landscape around Salamanca, flat in the immediate vicinity and to the west, but rising sharply to east and south, towards the Gredos range, the Sierra de Béjar, and the abrupt hills of Las Hurdes, arguably Spain's most backward area in those days. This was the countryside that Unamuno knew well through frequent excursions, for example to the shrine of Our Lady found in the Sierra de la Peña de Francia, beautifully described in an intensely personal account in *Andanzas y visiones españolas* ['Spanish Walks and Views']. This parched, rocky landscape, the very opposite of luxuriant, and different too from the green hills of the Basque Country that Unamuno knew in his youth, conveys permanence, constancy, immutability, and a strong sense of history (as in poem No. 20 about the 'Rock of France'). Sometimes this history is itself metaphorical, as occurs in the poem about the lake at San Martín de Castañeda (No. 21) in which the submerged belfry of the church of Valverde de Lucerna tolls for past generations of villagers.

Unamuno's interior world, then, is often expressed through familiar exterior images, or perhaps it might be more correct to say that the process of constructing exterior images itself evokes spiritual worlds. One image we notice, for example, is that of labourers toiling in the fields who turn to look up at the sky in hope. This is after all a perfectly ordinary and common occurrence. But in Unamuno's poems the soil and the sky are made to exist conjointly, reaching out to each other, as if the human world aspired to the spiritual dimension of the divine world, and the divine world aspired to the concrete expression of the human one. This Thomist conjunction of body and spirit, the idea that each one needs the other to express itself, is reproduced almost literally, making use of the earth and sky images, in poem No. 1088 of the *Cancionero*: 'si el cuerpo quiere ser cielo en la tierra, / el alma quiere ser tierra en el cielo' ['if the body wants to be heaven on earth, / the soul wants to be earth in heaven']. This image of earth and sky reaching out to each other is found even in poems that have little to do with landscape as occurs in the ballad 'Waiting' (poem No. 12), in which there seems to be a line of communication (literally a 'sendero' or lane) between the dead in their graves and the stars in the firmament. This sense of communion between the human and the divine worlds is not just a feature of Unamuno's poetry but of his entire philosophy.[6]

Rivers of course appear frequently, but again they are not simply metaphors for life; they are very often real rivers, especially those most closely linked to Unamuno's experience, the Nervión, the Tormes, and the Bidasoa, associated respectively with youth in Bilbao, maturity in Salamanca, and exile in Hendaye. Unamuno recalls Jorge Manrique's well-known comparison of human life with a river ending in the sea of death, but Unamuno goes further because he sees the sea not just as the

---

6   In the sixteenth century such a mystical or quasi-mystical sense of the divine was regarded with suspicion by the Catholic Church and many who held such views – which of course circumvented the Church as mediatrix – were punished by the Inquisition for heresy. In the twentieth century Unamuno was repeatedly denounced as a heretic by the Spanish hierarchy, even to the extent of having the newly-published *Cancionero* collection of poetry confiscated by Franco's police nearly twenty years after his death. 'Nihil novum sub sole', as Unamuno liked to say.

death of the river but also as its source: 'downstream comes / fecund cloud and rain and flood', as he writes in poem No. 13. In poem No. 18 he identifies his life closely with the river Tormes and the surrounding countryside as his years in Salamanca flow by inexorably like the waters of the nearby river along whose banks he liked to walk. And in poem No. 19 he sees the river as a fount of wisdom accumulated through millenia of existence as it flows through the lands of St Teresa and Fray Luis.

Writing

It is scarcely surprising that a man so utterly dedicated to writing should have entertained a theory about this activity.[7] For Unamuno any book, when expressing something deeply felt, was an almost sacred artefact, the word made flesh. Indeed he changed the opening words of St John's Gospel, 'In the beginning was the Word' to 'In the beginning was the Book'. In the first instance the Book is of course the Old Testament, written to give a sense of pride and identity to a people subjected to two lengthy periods of captivity and enslavement. But by extension it applies to all books or literary compositions that explore facets of the human condition or seek answers to questions about ourselves and our relationships. A book – Unamuno uses the word loosely to include all genres including 'non-artistic' genres such as philosophy and historiography – contains the essence of its maker, and it transmits that essence to the reader in an act that is both revelation and communion, for in reconstructing that essence the reader has to dig within his or her own resources to grasp the author's consciousness or sense of identity. A book is a mirror of both writers and readers, but it is a mirror with the capacity to transform, because a book exists in the mind and we interact with it as we interact with other minds. The book satisfies our hunger for knowledge, for understanding our world and our role in it. The pursuit of 'pure poetry', poetry detached from any kind of intrusive preoccupation, the goal of the Nobel laureate Juan Ramón Jiménez and other contemporaries, made little sense to Unamuno. For him, writing in general and poetry in particular, was first and foremost self-revelation, both to himself and to others, and at the

---

7   This is a major topic with endless ramifications which I have studied at length elsewhere (*Unamuno's Theory of the Novel* [Oxford: Legenda, 2014]), but I must here limit my comments to the barest essentials.

same time a way of reaching out beyond one's temporal and physical limitations. His verse, he says, is a 'mirror of humanity' (poem No. 34), an ambitious attempt to capture everything that is important about the human situation. There is therefore an intimate connection between text and person. To write is to read oneself, and to read is similarly a creative and re-creative endeavour, as he often expresses (*e.g.* in poems No. 10 and No. 11). Every poem is an expression of a living body and carries something of that pulsating being that created it; hence Unamuno's reluctance to excise even the most trivial composition. Everything that he wrote he saw as stemming from and adding to his personality. His legend, as he called it, literally the way he was 'read', perceived or thought of, emanated from his writing or self-expression.

The poet's task begins as a dialogue with himself, he tells us in an ingenious poem which describes the process of creation, a *mise en abyme* much more typical of the novel (poem No. 35). The idea that lies at the heart of a poem emerges from the rhythm or melody that begins to take flight as the poet searches for the poem's 'incarnation in the flesh of words', an obvious religious image. Find the right words and the poem will develop a direction, a sense of purpose, a melody that stays alive by searching for its own wings in the world of words. In the end we do not know which is more real, the words or the poem, in what is of course the eternal question of the philosophy of universals (whether they truly exist or whether only their separate ingredients exist).[8] Does a melody exist, or do only the separate musical notes exist? A poem conveys a particular vision, but in this particular case the poet confesses that he does not know where that vision comes from. 'Melody' also occurs in poem No. 34, where it stands for the reconciliation of opposites, for an overarching truth that is impossible to achieve through reasoned argument. A poem, then, would appear to have its own way of providing insight over and above the words employed.

For all his training as a philologist and his prodigious output, the world of words was not one that Unamuno took for granted or found amenable. Indeed the opposite, since he often complained of the difficulty encountered

---

8   This is the theme of poem No. 42: what is more real, the natural world, represented by a frog searching for a mate, or Kant's highly abstract *Critique of Pure Reason* which explains how we perceive such a world? *Mutatis mutandis* this is applicable to all scientific explanations of our universe.

in trying to express one's own meanings and personal outlook with words that seemed to want to express a meaning all of their own. In one of his poems from *Poesías sueltas* he goes as far as to say that his words do not belong to him but that he belongs to his words. This difficulty in taming language is expressed poetically in 'The Cruel Word' (poem No. 37), in which he says that words cheat him of his intended meaning. He feels trapped behind an iron grille which stops him from breaking loose and expressing what he wants to express in a way unconstrained by the pre-existing values of words handed down to him. What he felt he needed was a language 'free of all defacement', as he says in 'The Word as Symbol' (poem No. 38), a sort of Edenic language free of the contamination of a fallen world. Such a language, which in this poem he associates with the divine, would allow us to see what is real about our world and our existence. Words would denominate not objects but signs, and in so doing would let us perceive our ultimate destiny. But despite his complaints about our language forcing us to think and express ourselves in certain ways, there is no doubt that it provided him with a medium through which he could be enormously creative. Even when writing about life as endless repetition, as he does in 'Philosophemes' (poem No. 47), he finds an extraordinarily rich and imaginative way of putting the idea across, imaginative even in the sense that the poem is a sustained succession of images on the biblical theme of 'nothing new under the sun', except that here the sun is what is new 'in every old day'. Unamuno's inventiveness with 'old' words is of course the mark of his genius.

Mortality

At the very centre of Unamuno's existential philosophy lies the question of our ineluctable mortality, an aspect of our existence that he found hard to accept, and the overcoming of which he placed at the heart of humanity's religious history, as he explains in *The Tragic Sense of Life*, tragic in the sense that we cannot seem to find decisive answers to our questions or satisfying assurances for our aspirations. The hankering for survival, for living on with our loved ones which is such a persistent feature of Unamuno's writing, has been converted by a number of Spanish scholars into so-called 'Erostratism', the idea of achieving immortality through art (rather than through Herostratus's nefarious act of setting fire to the temple of Artemis at Ephesus). But we must be careful to distinguish between our own re-creation of a dead person's way of thinking when we read or contemplate that person's work and that dead person continuing to live through his or her own work. The latter can only be, at best, a metaphorical living. Unamuno himself several times expressed scepticism about this form of living on. In poem No. 39, for example, he takes the Roman poet Horace to task for writing 'Non omnis moriar multaque pars mei vitabit Libitinam', ['Not all of me will die, for much of me will evade Libitina' (goddess of death)], by which Horace meant that in his poetry he had created a monument that would eternalize him and defy oblivion. Unamuno reminds the Roman poet and us that art too will die one day. For Unamuno living required a body, not a book. The loss of the body meant the loss of life. This is in fact a perfectly orthodox Christian position to take and is in accordance with the greatest of Christian theologians, St Thomas Aquinas, who taught that our lives will only be resumed when God resurrects our bodies and that in the meantime our disembodied souls must remain in a state of suspension.[9] The work of art, then, cannot restore the dead individual to any kind of consciousness; only God can do that. What it does is to enable us, the living, to share the artist's vision, that person's individuality or uniqueness, an idea expressed in what must be one of Unamuno's most beautiful poems, 'Reading the Living Book of a Dead Friend' (No. 11), effective in the simplicity of its expression and moving in its feeling of closeness to the dead friend: reading the words of the now dead author helps the reader to recapture his spirit and thus to recognize what they have in common, and what they have in common, at least in this poem, is a deep sense of God's presence. In poem No. 10, also on this theme, Unamuno expresses his regret that his poem should outlive him: 'That you should outlive me my song! / O works of mine, works which belong / to my soul's fertility, / why don't you give your life to me?' The poem reminds the reader that the poet no longer is: 'It is my song, it is not me / that carries in this world / the shadow of my ghostly self, / of my abysmal nullity.' Not only is the poet reduced to nothing, but the poem too will meet its end when there is no-one to read it, as the closing lines indicate.

The question of art and immortality is thus not really a matter of pursuing

---

9   This is the Thomist doctrine referred to by Unamuno in the quotation from poem No. 1088 in the *Cancionero* cited above.

one through the medium of the other. In a way it is even more basic, for it is tied to Unamuno's own psychological make-up. Unamuno, who started publishing at the age of fifteen, admitted that he had a deep-seated need for self-expression and felt a compulsion to write in order to find or assert his individuality. This is obviously a psychological phenomenon rather than a religious or artistic one. But Unamuno had his own way of looking at it. He saw his obsessive need for self-expression as a creative urge, as *poiesis*, creative production. He took poet in its original Greek meaning of maker rather than its narrower meaning of writer of verses, and he drew an analogy with the supreme *poietes*, God, and His self-expression through the creation of the universe. The poet's creative urge is in its own limited way a reflection of divine creativity. Just as God is not commensurate with His creation but is nevertheless present in it, a poet is not to be confused with his or her creation but nevertheless retains some vestige of himself or herself in it. The creative analogy is of course suggested by the Bible, which tells us that God created man in His image and also that He invited Adam to participate in the creation by conferring names on the created objects. But the analogy also creates a conundrum. Why should a creator destroy what he has so painstakingly created? Life, anyone's life, is a free gift, not a necessity. Why is it taken away? Or as Unamuno put it in one of his poems from the *Cancionero*, 'Oración a Santa Rita' ['Prayer to Saint Rita'], based on a children's ditty, 'Abogada de imposibles, / Santa Rita la bendita, / la vida es un don del cielo, / lo que se da no se quita' ['Blessed Saint Rita, who pleads / on behalf of the lost cause, / life is a heavenly gift / not to be taken from us']. Unamuno, who refused to 'destroy' any of his creations (his revisions typically led to additions, not excisions), could not explain why something that had been freely created should be returned to nothingness.

The most common theme by far in Unamuno's poetry is man's mortality and the natural resistance to it. Unamuno repeatedly takes up a position of protest against finitude, as we observe in the closing lines of poems No. 14 and No. 17, as well as in the final poem of his life (No. 50). At times this protest is tempered by hope of a renewed existence, and this hope is typically expressed through the beneficial influence of others, his children trustingly asleep, the reassuring gaze of his wife Concha, the inspiring words of a great writer. More generally there is something of the Romantic protest still extant in Unamuno, but in the latter it usually adopts the form of a dialogue with a transcendent being and takes its cue from Jesus Christ's words on the cross 'My God, my God, why have you forsaken me?'. Unamuno was no atheist, but his God is one that leaves us to our own devices, who offers us no assurance of immortality, and who listens to us impassively. Much of his poetry is a dialogue not with God, as he would like, but with himself, a dialogue, that is, between the self that carries an intense and mysterious desire for perdurance and the self that sees no very convincing reason why this perdurance will take place, between a timeless God carried within and a pressing and time-bound consciousness, between a vision of eternity and a distressing conviction of finitude. Unamuno found many ways of expressing this deep contradiction in himself, and the clash breaks through even in poems that are ostensibly about other subjects.

The rejection of unmitigated, absolute mortality implies the rejection of reason, or more accurately its relegation from the position of dominance it had come to occupy in the eighteenth and nineteenth centuries, since it is reason that tells us that our lives must irretrievably end. If we are capable of imagining other worlds, why should we give priority to the perishable world that comes to us through our senses and ordered through our reason? Our imagination, our intuition, and our creative capacity amount to a dimension of our being that is as real as our reason. This is the idea behind poem No. 16, in which Unamuno declares that he will never subject God to the tyranny of reason. Rational belief in God would be too easy and comfortable. Instead, Unamuno wants to believe combatively against our reason and through our imagination. We can now see why *poiesis* meant so much to Unamuno. It is this creative urge, which His creatures have inherited from their Creator, that promises to save us from nothingness. Indeed Unamuno went so far as to see human creativity and poetry itself as the revelation of a world beyond the strict limits of reason. The urge to poetize is a pointer to our divine nature, of our 'right to be' as he eloquently affirms in poem No. 14. Unamuno meets his Maker face to face to stake his claim as co-creator.

The Translation

We can divide the use of language into two broad areas: communicative and creative. The communicative function serves to convey information about our circumstances and our world, a world that we take to be real and recognizable. This communicative function is most common in spoken language. The creative function by contrast is much more common in written language. Language gives us the capacity to create worlds that go beyond the immediate experiences provided by our five senses. It enables us to create parallel worlds, that is to say, worlds that are 'unreal' in the sense of having no identifiable presence outside the realm of language. A great deal of our cultural heritage would not exist were it not for language, and especially written language.

Unamuno started his long career as a philologist while in his teens, and for a time considered the spoken language as the medium of the transmission of a people's cultural traditions, since after all widespread literacy is a relatively modern phenomenon. But he gradually modified his views to give greater importance to writing, firstly because writing not only gathers and transmits vestiges of orality but it perdures much more visibly and reliably than speech (we know how people wrote hundreds, even thousands, of years ago, but we know very little about how they spoke); and secondly because he came to see the creative function of language as of paramount importance, and this creativity is expressed far more deeply through writing than through speech. For Unamuno any great writer is a poet, irrespective of the genre he cultivated, because he saw the work of the poet with the eyes of a professor of Greek, and as I mentioned earlier *poiesis* means creation. The supreme poet or maker is of course God, who – as recorded in the Book of Genesis – named as he created, that is to say he created linguistically, and then invited Adam to do the same. Among the great 'poets' Unamuno had a special affection or admiration for those who really were poets and not simply creators in prose, writers such as Shakespeare, Goethe, Leopardi, Carducci, Wordsworth, Browning, or Antero de Quental, writers who had a distinctive voice or personal vision. And it is this personal vision that characterizes all of Unamuno's work, but especially, because of its undoubted consistency in such a versatile writer, his poetry.

It is precisely this personal way of looking at the world that a translator must strive to capture in the renderings into another language. My approach eschews literal translations except where such translation offers a comfortable rendering in English. In general, then, I have adopted a much freer approach than one would in a prose translation. My aim has been to give priority to the tone and sense of each poem and to treat lexicon and syntax as secondary issues. A reader familiar with both languages will have no trouble in finding lexical divergences, omissions, or even additions in my renderings, but these are of course relatively minor adjustments which should not alter the sense of the poem taken as a whole. They are a requirement of the poetic structure, which is scarcely a factor in prose translation. Poetic structure is more idiosyncratic, personal, even contrived, in the sense of unusual. Such contrivance or departure from the norm is part and parcel of creative inventiveness and must somehow be preserved rather than converted into conventional expression. In the case of Unamuno there is the added consideration that with some exceptions he is working within traditional poetic forms, and this attachment to familiar forms, which of course affects the flow of the poem, the way it asks to be read, needs to be taken into account, though not slavishly reproduced. In practice this means that where Unamuno uses rhyme my translation also uses rhyme, though not necessarily 'rich' or 'strong' rhyme; and where Unamuno uses regular metre my version also uses regular metre, though not necessarily the same metre. To reproduce both the rhyme and the metre of the original is scarcely practical. Poem No. 19, 'To the River Tormes', for example, retains the abba rhyme scheme of the original but the hendecasyllabic verse changes to a decasyllabic one. I should add that Unamuno was prone to take liberties with metre, especially in his earlier poetry, and I have occasionally felt justified in doing the same. This applies even more to stress: Unamuno quite simply did not observe conventional stress in his use of the hendecasyllable.

Assonance, extremely common in Spanish poetry and relatively easy to achieve because of the limit of standard vowel sounds to five, carries its own problems in translation, given the large variation in English vowel sounds, but to an extent this applies to rhyme as well, though discrepancies in this case are masked by strong consonants. The differences in traditional poetic forms in English and Spanish discourage the search for precise equivalents, and I have not followed such a path. Instead my approach has been pragmatic and adaptive. In most cases the decision as to rhyme and metre has been made on the basis of the first few verses of the poem. Once the early verses or first quatrain have been translated it is a matter of sticking to the form employed. The old-fashioned distinction between content and form ('fondo y forma' in

Spanish) which still plagued the study of literature in the middle decades of the twentieth century was eventually superseded by the insistence that form is an integral part of the content and cannot be separated from it. The truth, if truth there be in these affairs of the mind, is probably somewhere in-between. Language is a flexible tool, and one can sometimes say the same thing in a different way, or say a different thing using the same words in a different context or tone (what else, if not, is irony?).

The most obvious challenge one faces in translating Unamuno is how to reflect the complex personality that comes through in his poems, the ferment of his ideas, the way in which he mixes concepts, sentiments, anxieties, literary and historical references, people, places, landscapes and seascapes, philological and philosophical-cum-religious reflexions. Of course the degree of complexity varies, but even relatively straightforward poems such as those that describe landscapes, monuments, or local products (*e.g.* No. 18, 'Land of the Tormes') will usually end with one or two verses of deeply personal reflexion which must be accounted for in the translation even though a literal rendering is out of the question for reasons of form or register: 'siglos de vida que se me fueron' clearly cannot be rendered simply as 'centuries of my life that have slipped from my grasp', which is what it means. Even the famous ode to Salamanca (poem No. 17), impersonal to an unusual degree, ends with a plaintive 'remember me' cry, through which Unamuno appeals for his presence to be recorded in precisely the way that Jesus asked his disciples to keep a memory of him. Unamuno of course does not mention Jesus's 'do this in memory of me', and neither can the translator; he can only hope that the reader will perceive the implied reference.

But it is not the expression of personal sentiments that provide the biggest challenge; indeed the poems which deal with Unamuno's feelings towards his family are easier to reproduce because such feelings are universal and admit of comparable expression in the target language. Those that try to convey more abstract or philosophical quandaries are in some ways harder because a greater degree of precision is called for: too free a rendering may miss the point, and a too slavish one will produce a stilted version. There is a delicate balance to be struck here and each case has to be considered anew. In poem No. 42, 'Kant and the Frog', for example, I have kept close to the original in order to bring out the stark contrast between the world of human concepts and the world of nature which is the point of the poem. In poem No. 45, 'Entropy', on the other hand I have given myself much more freedom in order to allow for an unusual rhyme scheme, but I trust the sense of the original is nevertheless retained.

As the philologist that he was, Unamuno wrote many poems on language (there is a very large number in the *Cancionero*). Most of them I regard as untranslatable because they rely on punning for their effect. I have nevertheless tried to give some indication of Unamuno's interest in language and expression by translating a number of poems whose theme is essentially linguistic, or at least has to do with the question of a poet's self-expression. Poem No. 36, 'The Vibrant Word', has a fairly free English version, but the assonance of the even verses in the original has been strengthened by the use of rhyme. Poem No. 37, 'The Cruel Word', on the other hand has been given a more literal translation but rhyme has been sacrificed. This is an almost inevitable choice in translating poetry (closer without rhyme, freer with), and one or the other approach is a matter of preference or experiment. The translation of poem No. 38, 'The Word as Symbol', is a kind of halfway house: rhyming has been retained but changed to the even verses of each quatrain (instead of the complicated abca, bcab, dede, of the original); the simplified rhyme scheme allows for a relatively closer translation. In any case what must obviously be respected in this kind of conceptual poetry is the idea the poet is putting across, in this particular case (No. 38) that language confers a reality to human existence that would be totally lacking without it; language is not reality but *our* reality.

By way of conclusion I would recall the well-known fact that translation involves a continuous choice between fidelity to the source language and fidelity to the natural cadences and phraseology of the target language. What one says or writes in one language is not necessarily what one says or writes in another. My experience of participating in various postgraduate translation courses in the 1990s and early 2000s suggests to me that the general philosophy was to prioritise the original source language over the target language; inventive translations were discouraged on the grounds that the author of a text was the ultimate and unquestionable authority and the translator had no right to usurp that authority. My own philosophy is rather the reverse: that provided the general sense of the original utterance is retained, the target language must be given priority over the source language. Translations are not done, or at any rate not done primarily, for the sake of authors but for the sake of readers. I would say that this applies to prose translation, but even more to the translation of poetry. After all, a poet, like any other person, does not exist purely for him or herself; he or she exists, and much more so, for others. And as it happens it was Unamuno himself who did much to promulgate that idea. 'Lector, el poeta aquí eres tú' ['Dear reader, it is you who is the poet'], he says in the closing lines of his prologue to the *Cancionero*. For him, his readers always had the last word. This is indeed the very theme from one of his early poems, 'Cuando yo ya sea viejo' ['When I am old', not included in this anthology], where we find the following lines:

> The soul which here I have disclosed
> will fall one day into the void;
> I will no longer hear my songs;
> it's you who will discern their tones.
> In them you will no doubt perceive
> what I myself cannot conceive,
> not even now that I write this,
> for you will see what I had missed.

Editions of Unamuno's Poetry

So far there have been three attempts to collect all of Unamuno's writings in one edition. None has succeeded. The first edition of the so-called *Obras completas* is that of 1958: Miguel de Unamuno, *Obras completas*, edited by Manuel García Blanco, 16 vols. (Madrid: Afrodisio Aguado/ Vergara 1958–64) (the poetry is in volumes 13–15). Most of Unamuno's known poems already appear in this edition. A revised version of these collected works appeared not long after the first version was completed: *Obras completas*, 6 vols (Madrid: Escelicer 1964–71) (the poetry is in volume 6). Errors abound in both versions.

The third attempt at a complete works is that known as the Biblioteca Castro edition: Miguel de Unamuno, *Obras completas*, edited by Ricardo Senabre, 10 vols (Madrid: Biblioteca Castro/Turner, 1995–2009) (the poetry appears in volumes 4 and 5, and the few poems that belong to *Andanzas y visiones españolas* appear in their rightful place in volume 6). This promised to be an improvement on the earlier versions, but in fact publication appears to have stopped in 2009 well short of completion. Although this edition has a more rational ordering and is today much more accessible, it is in some respects the least satisfactory of all, such are the errors that have crept in, from a wrong d.o.b. for Unamuno himself, to mis-attributions (*e.g.* Aristophanes's *The Wasps* attributed to Aristotle), and numerous mis-renderings (*e.g.* 'bragando' for 'bregando', 'número' for 'noúmeno' and so on). One suspects the text has been prepared by a team of inexperienced young editors inadequately supervised by the general editor. The best one can say is that all the known poetry seems to be there.

The original publications of the poems, as detailed at the beginning of this Introduction, are difficult to find (some but not all may be found in the Bibliteca Nacional, Madrid, and similarly in the Casa-Museo in Salamanca), so reliance on one or other version of the *Obras completas* has become the norm. But there is another accessible and reliable collection: Miguel de Unamuno, *Poesía completa*, edited by Ana Suárez Miramón, 4 vols (Madrid: Alianza Editorial, 1987–89). This is a careful edition and worth checking for possible variants. I have consulted these various editions and corrected obvious misprints and mis-punctuations.

Many of Unamuno's poems were not given titles. Where I have provided a title I have placed it in square brackets above the Spanish version of the poem.

The fifty short commentaries included after the poems are intended to contextualize the poems, to point to their links with Unamuno's life and/or thought. They also contain some clarifications of allusions within the poems where this has been deemed helpful. On the whole Unamuno's verse, like his prose, is free of obscurities, and the sense of what he is saying is nearly always perfectly apparent.

Acknowledgement

I am grateful to Don Miguel de Unamuno Adarraga and his literary agents Ute Körner for permission to publish the original Spanish version of Unamuno's poems.

SELECT CRITICAL BIBLIOGRAPHY

(1) In English

Garofalo, S. (1972) The Tragic Sense in the Poetry of Leopardi and Unamuno, *Symposium* 26, 197–211.

Krause, A. (1956) Unamuno and Tennyson, *Comparative Literature* 8.2, 122–35.

Flores Moreno, C. (2005–08) Nature Imagined in S. T. Coleridge's 'Meditative Poems' and Miguel de Unamuno's *Poesías, Journal of English Studies* (Universidad de La Rioja) 5–6 (2005–08), 83–103.

Flores Moreno, C. (2010a) Contemplative Unamuno: The Presence of S. T. Coleridge's 'Musings' in Miguel de Unamuno's Poetics, *Comparative Critical Studies* 7.1, 41–65.

Flores Moreno, C. (2010b) 'Imported Seeds': The Role of William Wordsworth in Miguel de Unamuno's Poetic Renewal. In *Romanticism and the Anglo-Hispanic Imaginary*, edited by J. M. Almeida (Amsterdam: Brill/Rodopi), pp. 249–71.

Flores Moreno, C. (2011) William Blake's Legacy in Miguel de Unamuno's Mature Poetry and Poetics, *Estudios Ingleses de la Universidad Complutense* 19, 89–104.

McCargar, W. K. (1980) *The Poetry of Miguel de Unamuno* (Madison: University of Wisconsin Press).

Valdés, M. J. (1970) Archetype and Recreation: A Comparative Study of William Blake and Miguel de Unamuno, *University of Toronto Quarterly* 40, 58–72.

Valdés, M. J. (1975) The Aesthetic Relationship of William Blake and Miguel de Unamuno. In *Proceedings of the Sixth Congress of the International Comparative Literature Association* (Stuttgart: Bieber), pp. 809–11.

Young, H. T. (1964) *The Victorious Expression. A Study of Four Contemporary Spanish poets: Unamuno, Machado, Jiménez, García Lorca* (Madison: University of Wisconsin Press).

(2) In Spanish

Alvar, M. (1964) *Acercamientos a la poesía de Unamuno* (Santa Cruz de Tenerife: Universidad de La Laguna).

Álvarez Castro, L. (2009) Miguel de Unamuno, ¿poeta vanguardista? El diálogo entre teoría y praxis lírica en el *Cancionero, Bulletin of Spanish Studies* LXXXVI:2 , 205–25.

Beuchot, M. (2011) Poesía y ontología en Miguel de Unamuno. In *Unamuno y nosotros*, edited by Juan Carlos Moreno Romo (Barcelona: Anthropos), pp. 155–67.

Díez de Revenga, F. J. (1989) Unamuno poeta: en torno al *Cancionero* como poesía de senectud. In *Actas del congreso internacional cincuentenario de Unamuno*, edited by D. Gómez Molleda (Salamanca: Ediciones Universidad de Salamanca), pp. 441–46.

García Blanco, M. (1954) *Don Miguel de Unamuno y sus poesías* (Salamanca: Acta Salmanticensia).

García Blanco, M. (1975) Introduction to Miguel de Unamuno, *Poemas de los pueblos de España* (Madrid: Cátedra), pp. 13–38.

García de la Concha, V. (2000) Unamuno y la poética de la modernidad. In *Tu mano es mi destino. Congreso internacional Miguel de Unamuno*, edited by Cirilo Flórez Miguel (Salamanca: Ediciones Universidad de Salamanca), pp. 167–83.

Imizcoz Beúnza, T. (1996) *La teoría poética de Miguel de Unamuno* (Pamplona: Ediciones Universidad de Navarra).

Kock, J. de. (1968) *Introducción al 'Cancionero' de Miguel de Unamuno* (Madrid: Gredos).

Kock, J. de. (1989) *Cancionero* y la poesía. In *Actas del congreso internacional cincuentenario de Unamuno*, edited by D. Gómez Molleda (Salamanca: Ediciones Universidad de Salamanca), pp. 121–30.

La poesía de Miguel de Unamuno (1987) edited by J. A. Ascunce Arrieta (San Sebastián: Universidad de Deusto).

Miguel de Unamuno, poeta (2003) edited by Javier Blasco, Pilar Celma and Ramón González (Valladolid: Universidad de Valladolid).

Paez Martín, J. J. (2003) Una tensión lírica unamuniana. In *Miguel de Unamuno. Estudio sobre su obra I*, edited by Ana Chaguaceda Toledano (Salamanca: Ediciones Universidad de Salamanca), pp. 13–26.

Paoli, R. (1997) Introduction to Miguel de Unamuno, *Antología poética* (Madrid: Espasa).

Pulido Rosa, I. (2003) Elementos originales y modelos constructivos en la poética de Miguel de Unamuno. In *Miguel de Unamuno. Estudio sobre su obra I*, edited by Ana Chaguaceda Toledano (Salamanca: Ediciones Universidad de Salamanca), pp. 27–35.

Pulido Rosa, I. (2000) Innovaciones poéticas en Miguel de Unamuno. In *Tu mano es mi destino. Congreso internacional Miguel de Unamuno*, edited by Cirilo Flórez Miguel (Salamanca: Ediciones Universidad de Salamanca), pp. 395–404.

Sainz Rodríguez, P. (1986) Unamuno y la poesía. In *Volumen-Homenaje Cincuentenario a Miguel de Unamuno* (Salamanca: Casa-Museo Unamuno), pp. 495–500.

Sotelo Vázquez, A. (1987) Miguel de Unamuno y la forja de la poesía desnuda de Juan Ramón Jiménez, *Hispanic Review* 55, 195–212.

Ynduráin, F. (1969) Unamuno en su poética y como poeta. In *Clásicos modernos* (Madrid: Gredos), pp. 59–125.

Zardoya, C. (1961) *Poesía española contemporánea. Estudios temáticos y estilísticos* (Madrid: Guadarrama), pp. 91–178.

Biographies

There are two recent and highly informative biographies of Unamuno in Spanish. The first of these is a general biography. The second focuses more narrowly on Unamuno's professional life at the University of Salamanca:

Rabaté, C. and Rabaté J. C. (2009) *Miguel de Unamuno. Biografía* (Madrid: Taurus).

Blanco Prieto, F. (2011) *Unamuno: profesor y rector de la universidad de Salamanca* (Salamanca: Hergar/Antema).

For those who cannot read Spanish the following biography is less complete but still serviceable:

Rudd, M. (1963) *The Lone Heretic. A Biography of Miguel de Unamuno y Jugo* (Austin: University of Texas Press).

I

FAMILY AND HOME

1 [VOLVIENDO A CASA]

Cuando he llegado de noche
todo dormía en mi casa,
todo en la paz del silencio
recostado en la confianza.
Sólo se oía el respiro,
respiro de grave calma,
de mis hijos que dormían
sueño que la vida alarga.
Y era oración su respiro,
respirando el sueño oraban,
con la conciencia en los brazos
del Padre que el sueño ampara.
Eres, sueño, el anticipo
de la vida que no acaba,
vida pura que respira
debajo de la que pasa.

1 **RETURNING HOME**

When I arrived at home last night
I felt the silence long and deep.
Amidst the peaceful quietude
all were trustingly asleep.
The only sound that could be heard
was of my children as they slept,
the breathing of that restful sleep
that gives our lives a longer thread.
Their breathing was an act of prayer,
in which they dreamt their future breath,
while the Father ever watchful
looked after their wakefulness.
Oh sleep, you are the premonition
of a life which will remain,
a pure life which breathes forever
below that which fades away.

2 [EL HOGAR]

Llueve desde tus ojos alegría
sobre mi casa.
De no haber anudado nuestras vidas,
¿es que yo hoy viviría?
Estos mis ocho hijos que me has dado
¡son mis raíces!
Aquel viejo enemigo de mi pecho
habríame vencido.
O en un rincón de un claustro,
en una triste celda,
en brega con la fe que se me escapa,
luchando con la acedía.
O en un rincón de un camposanto oscuro,
¡allí, en lo no bendito,
donde se guarda a los que no supieron
esperar a la muerte!

Pero mira cómo he hecho
de este mi hogar en que tus ojos ríen
un claustro, un monasterio,
y un campo santo,
¡dulce reposadero de los vivos!
Aquí la paz del claustro y de la tumba
con alegría y vida.
¡Aquí al sentirme renacer en otros,
al oír en sus risas
cantar de mi niñez viejos recuerdos,
levanto el corazón a nuestro Padre
mientras aprendo
a esperar a la muerte!

2 **HOME**

Your eyes let fall a joyful rain
upon my dwelling place.
Had we not joined our lives would I
be still alive today?
Eight children you have given me,
they have become my roots!
I might have been defeated
by my ancient enemy.
Or else in some monastic corner,
in a dismal cell I'd be,
wrestling with a faith that flees,
depression held at bay.
Or stowed away in a dark grave
in unconsecrated ground
where those who could not wait for death
are laid down out of bounds.

But see how I have turned my house
before your smiling eyes
into a cloistered monastery,
a holy cemetery
that offers rest to those alive!
Here is the joyful, living
peace both of cloister and of grave.
Others make me feel reborn,
for singing echoes of my youth
in their laughter I discern.
And I lift my heart to God
whilst to await
my death I learn!

3 DULCE SILENCIOSO PENSAMIENTO

Sweet silent thought.
Shakespeare, Sonnet XXX.

En el fondo las risas de mis hijos;
yo sentado al amor de la camilla;
Heródoto me ofrece rica cilla
del eterno saber y entre acertijos

de la Pitia venal, cuentos prolijos,
realce de la eterna maravilla
de nuestro sino. Frente a mí en su silla
ella cose, y teniendo un rato fijos

mis ojos de sus ojos en la gloria
digiero los secretos de la historia,
y en la paz santa que mi casa cierra,

al tranquilo compás de un quieto aliento,
ara en mí, como un manso buey la tierra,
el dulce silencioso pensamiento.

3 SWEET SILENT THOUGHT

Sweet silent thought.
Shakespeare, Sonnet XXX.

The laughter of my children over there,
while I sit by the warmth of the brazier
and savour the rich, eternal wisdom
of Herodotus, and in the midst of riddles

from the Delphic Pythia, endless stories
that mark the ceaseless wonder of our fate.
Opposite me she sits and sews, her eyes
fixed on eternal things, and for a while

my eyes alight on hers and through them
I absorb the secrets of all history,
and in the holy peace that girds my house,

in measured step with gentle breath, like
oxen ploughing the soil, there works
in me a sweet and silent thought.

4 AL NIÑO ENFERMO

Duerme flor de mi vida
duerme tranquilo,
que es del dolor el sueño
tu único asilo.

Duerme, mi pobre niño,
goza sin duelo
lo que te da la Muerte
como consuelo.

Como consuelo y prenda
de su cariño,
de que te quiere mucho,
mi pobre niño.

Pronto vendrá con ansia
de recogerte
la que te quiere tanto
la dulce Muerte.

Dormirás en sus brazos
el sueño eterno,
y para ti, mi niño,
no habrá ya invierno.

No habrá invierno ni nieve,
mi flor tronchada,
te cantará el silencio
dulce tonada.

Oh, que triste sonrisa
riza tu boca,

4 TO THE SICK CHILD

Sleep, sleep, little flower,
sleep undisturbed,
a sleep that relieves you
from endless hurt.

Sleep, sleep my poor child,
take without grief
the one consolation
that Death concedes.

As the comfort and token
of her concern,
of her caring for you,
my little bairn.

She yearns to take with her
your living breath,
so much does she love you,
sweet-natured Death.

In her arms you will rest
forever asleep,
and for you, my dear child,
dark days will cease.

No more winter nor snow,
my severed flower,
only a silent tune,
to chime the hours.

On your lips you are showing
a smile so sad,

tu corazón acaso
su mano toca.

Oh que sonrisa triste
tu boca riza,
¿que es lo que en sueños dices
a tu nodriza?

A tu nodriza eterna
siempre piadosa,
la Tierra en que en paz santa
todo reposa.

Cuando el sol se levante,
mi pobre estrella,
derretida en el alba
te irás con ella.

Morirás con la aurora,
flor de la Muerte,
te rechaza la vida.
¡Qué hermosa suerte!

El sueño que no acaba,
duerme tranquilo,
que es del dolor la Muerte
tu único asilo.

are her fingers touching
your heart perhaps?

Oh, what a sad smile
your lips betray.
To your dear nurse in dreams,
what do you say?

She will always be with you
your gentle nurse,
lying in the holy peace
of our Mother Earth.

When dawn approaches,
my little star,
you will melt in the sun
and go with her.

Dawn, flower of Death,
will take your hand
when life says farewell.
Oh happy chance!

A never-ending sleep
to give you rest;
from your pain the only rescue
is brought by Death.

5 [EN LA MUERTE DE CONCHA]

Pasó por el mundo al paso
de una espera de sosiego
y fue a acostarse –sin fuego–
en dulce luz del ocaso.

No hizo sombra a nadie; opuso
a todo revés sonrisa
y un día al salir de misa
halló a su hombre; compuso

hogar todo a Dios abierto
en cercado de humildad,
y en lo alto, en soledad,
faro del celeste puerto.

Fue una vida sin historia,
en lo eterno cimentada,
por el mundo de pasada
una vida todo gloria.

5 UPON THE DEATH OF CONCHA

In this world she lived her life
in a mood of quiet content,
undisturbed she closed her eyes
in the rays of a day's end.

No harsh word for foe nor friend,
a smile for every arduous test,
and coming out of church one day
she met her man and built her nest.

A home where God was welcome guest,
a haven of humility,
where heaven's lighthouse from above
assured celestial sanctuary.

Her life was not a history
for it belonged to timelessness;
in transient passage on this earth,
her life was bathed in godliness.

6 [EN MI ESTUDIO]

Es de noche, en mi estudio.
Profunda soledad; oigo el latido
de mi pecho agitado,
–es que se siente solo,
y es que se siente blanco de mi mente–
y oigo la sangre
cuyo leve susurro
llena el silencio.
Diríase que cae el hilo líquido
de la clepsidra al fondo.
Aquí, de noche, solo, éste es mi estudio;
los libros callan;
mi lámpara de aceite
baña en lumbre de paz estas cuartillas,
lumbre cual de sagrario;
los libros callan;
de los poetas, pensadores, doctos,
los espíritus duermen;
y ello es como si en torno me rondase
cautelosa la muerte.
Me vuelvo a ratos para ver si acecha,
escudriño lo oscuro,
trato de descubrir entre las sombras
su sombra vaga,
pienso en la angina;
pienso en mi edad viril; de los cuarenta
pasé ha dos años.
Es una tentación dominadora

6 IN MY STUDY

It is night time. In my study
I'm all alone. I can detect
an agitated beating from my chest
 – it feels itself alone, it feels
itself the target of my thoughts –
and I can hear the blood
whose muted whisper
saturates the silence.
I think of a clepsydra
with its liquid, falling thread.
Alone, at night, this is my den;
the books around me are hushed,
my oil lamp throws a gentle
light upon these sheets,
as if guarding the consecrated host.
The books stay mute: the souls
of learned men, philosophers
and poets sleep on, as if around me
death were cautiously
preparing to lay siege.
At intervals I turn to see if it is
lying in wait and scrutinize the dark,
trying to make out its shadowy presence
among the embracing shadows.
My thoughts turn to angina,
to my maturing years: two since
my fourth decade was done and gone.
It is a pressing thought

que aquí, en la soledad, es el silencio
quien me la asesta;
el silencio y las sombras.
Y me digo: «Tal vez cuando muy pronto
vengan para anunciarme
que me espera la cena,
encuentren aquí un cuerpo
pálido y frío
–la cosa que fui yo, este que espera–
como esos libros, silencioso y yerto,
parada ya la sangre
yeldándose en las venas,
el pecho silencioso
bajo la dulce luz del blando aceite,
lámpara funeraria».
Tiemblo de terminar estos renglones
que no parezcan
extraño testamento,
más bien presentimiento misterioso
del allende sombrío,
dictados por el ansía
de vida eterna.
Los terminé y aún vivo.

with which silence assails me
when alone;
the silence and the shadows.
And to myself I say: 'The time is near
perhaps, when they come in to announce
that supper is being served,
only to find find a body here
that's white and cold
– the object that was I, this one who waits –
like those books over there, silent and stiff,
when the blood has ceased to flow
and gels within the veins,
when the chest has fallen silent
under the oil lamp's gentle glow,
now the candle of a corpse.'
I fear to bring these lines to a close
lest they appear to be a strange
last will and testament;
mysterious omen, rather,
of a bleak beyond
dictated by a yen
to live forever.
Yet they are done, and I live on.

7 [EL NIÑO Y EL MUÑECO]

El niño se creía sin testigos,
dibujando en el hule
que cubría la mesa;
trazaba en ella un *tío* primitivo,
al modo de los toscos
diseños de las cuevas en que el hombre
luchara con el oso cavernario.
Y mientras animaba
los rasgos del dibujo prehistórico
cantaba bajo:
«Soy de carne, soy de carne, no pintado,
soy de carne, soy de carne, verdadero».
¡Maravilla del arte!
¡Hacía hablar al *tío*
y proclamar la realidad viviente!
¿Hace acaso otra cosa
el Artista Supremo,
al recrearse, niño eterno, en su obra?

7 THE CHILD AND THE DOLL

The child thought he was unseen
as he doodled on the cloth
that covered the table top.
He sketched a crude figurine
like those primitive depictions
in which cavemen drew a scene
of their hunting expeditions.
And while he experimented
with his prehistoric drawing
in a hushed voice he was singing:
'I'm made of flesh, I'm not painted
on a page, I'm made of flesh,
I'm real.' Art is a prodigy!
He made the figure speak and claim
to be a living entity.
Is not the Supreme Artist saying
the same when he, eternal child,
remakes himself in his own drawing?

8 [LA PRESENCIA DE CONCHA]

Está aquí
más dentro de mí que yo mismo;
está aquí, sí;
en el divino abismo
en que huidiza eternidad se espeja
y en su inmortal sosiego
se sosiega mi queja.

¿Mas cómo pude andar tan ciego
que no vi que era su vista
la que hacía mi conquista,
día a día, del mundo que pasaba?
Ella vivía al día y me esperaba.
Y esperándome sigue en otra esfera;
la muerte es otra espera.

Aquel sosiego henchido de resignación;
sus ojos de silencio; aquel resón
del silencio de Dios a mi pregunta
mientras Él como a yunta
con mano todopoderosa
nos hizo arar la vida,
esta vida tan preciosa
en que creí no creer, pues me bastaba
su fe, la de ella, su fe henchida
de un santo no saber, de que sacaba
su simple y puro ver.

Que mientras me miraba
vi en su mirada el fondo de mi ser.

8 CONCHA'S PRESENCE

She is here,
inside me more than I myself;
yes, she is here,
in that divine abyss,
mirror of an elusory eternity,
and in her indestructible serenity
my plaint would be remiss.

How could I have been so blind
that I failed to realize
that it was her wondrous eyes
that saved me from the world of time?
Her days were one and all the same
waiting for me, and now again
she waits; death is a waiting game.

That peaceful look abrim with resignation,
that silent gaze, that faithful replication
of God's soundless response to every question,
whilst He with mighty hand
put us under the yoke
to plough the precious lands
of a life for me remote
because her faith embraced
us both, a faith unstained
by knowledge that enslaves,
a wisdom pure and plain.

And through her eyes I gazed
at my soul's secret domain.

En su regazo
de madre virginal
recogí con mi abrazo
las aguas del divino manantial
que pues no tuvo origen
no tendrá fin; aguas que rigen
nuestro santo contento,
la entrañada costumbre
que guarda eternidad en el momento.

¡Ay sus ojos, su lumbre
de recatada estrella
que arraiga en lo infinito del amor
y en que sentí la huella
de los pies del Señor!

Está aquí, está aquí, siempre conmigo
de todo aparentar al fin desnuda,
está aquí, al abrigo
del sino y de la duda.

In the pure bosom
of a vestal mother
I took with my embrace
the waters of a sacred spring
which left no earthly trace
of origin or end; waters that bring
to us divine felicity.
It is a habit of the soul
which in each movement holds eternity.

Oh, those eyes, that fire
of a retiring star
that shines with love's eternal light
in which I saw the mark
of the footprints of our Christ!

She is here, she is here, right by my side,
released from every role upon the stage,
she's here with me, no longer tyrannized
by questions and by fate.

II

GOD AND MORTALITY

9 [SILENCIOS VACÍOS]

¡Qué de silencios vacíos
sufrir bajo sombra amarga
entresacándole esquirlas
al esqueleto del alma!

¡Qué buscar en el silencio
–que es cuna de la palabra–
la verdad de Dios callado
a la puerta de su casa!

El hombre interior espera
–y esperar no da esperanza–
entrar en lo venidero
para salir de su nada.

En ensueño mero y mondo,
respiración sosegada
del aire del infinito;
no ve ni oye a Dios, le palpa.

Ciego y sordo el albedrío
envuelto en flores de cábala,
volo ergo existo, soñando
sueña que se sueña el alma.

9 EMPTY SILENCE

To suffer empty silence
under a bitter gloom,
removing hurtful splinters
from the soul's very womb!

To search amidst the stillness
– where the word has come to be –
for the truth of a mute God
at the door of his retreat.

The inner man's expecting
– though not with hopefulness –
to grasp what's in the future
to avoid his nothingness.

In the quiet of the night
he dreams of infinity,
neither sight nor sound of God,
yet feels his proximity.

Wrapped in mystic subtleties,
deaf and blind our free will lives,
and it dreams the soul's own dream,
volo ergo existo, it believes.

10 PARA DESPUÉS DE MI MUERTE

[...]
Oye tú que lees esto
después de estar yo en tierra,
cuando yo que lo he escrito
no puedo ya al espejo contemplarme;
¡oye y medita!
Medita, es decir, ¡sueña!

«Él, aquella mazorca
de ideas, sentimientos, emociones,
sensaciones, deseos, repugnancias,
voces y gestos,
instintos, raciocinios,
esperanzas, recuerdos,
y goces y dolores,
él, que se dijo yo, sombra de vida,
lanzó al tiempo esta queja
y hoy no la oye;
¡es mía ya, no suya!»

Sí, lector solitario, que así atiendes
la voz de un muerto,
tuyas serán estas palabras mías
que sonarán acaso
desde otra boca,
sobre mi polvo
sin que las oiga yo que soy su fuente.

Cuando yo ya no sea,
¡serás tú, canto mío!
Tú, voz atada a tinta,

10 **AFTER I CEASE TO BE**

[...]
Listen, you who are reading this
after in earth I have been laid,
when I who wrote it cannot now
in the mirror see my face;
listen and consider this!
Consider, that means, dream!

'He who was once a bundle
of ideas, sentiments, emotions,
of feelings, desires and revulsions,
of noisy speech, of silent motions,
of impulses and reasons,
of hopes and recollections,
of pleasure and of pain,
he who said "I", life's adumbration,
voiced this complaint
which now he does not hear;
it is no longer his but mine!'

Lone reader, you who listen
to the voice of a dead man,
these words of mine will have become
your words, whose sound will come
from another mouth which stands
above my dust and will not reach
their source in me.

When I can no longer breathe,
you, my song, will breathe for me!
You are a voice in ink confined,

aire encarnado en tierra,
doble milagro,
portento sin igual de la palabra,
portento de la letra,
¡tú nos abrumas!
¡Y que vivas tú más que yo, mi canto!
Oh, mis obras, mis obras,
hijas del alma,
¿por qué no habéis de darme vuestra vida?,
¿por qué a vuestros pechos
perpetuidad no ha de beber mi boca?
¡Acaso resonéis, dulces palabras,
en el aire en que floten
en polvo estos oídos
que ahora están midiéndoos el paso!
¡Oh tremendo misterio!
En el mar larga estela reluciente
de un buque sumergido.
¡Huellas de un muerto!

Oye la voz que sale de la tumba
y te dice al oído
este secreto:
«¡yo ya no soy, hermano!»
Vuelve otra vez, repite:
«¡yo ya no soy, hermano!»
Yo ya no soy; mi canto sobrevíveme
y lleva sobre el mundo
la sombra de mi sombra,
¡mi triste nada!
Me oyes tú, lector, yo no me oigo,
y esta verdad trivial, y que por serlo

a breath of air in clay enshrined,
a miracle in duplicate:
unique achievement of the word,
and marvel of the printed page.
You put us in the shade!
That you should outlive me my song!
Oh works of mine, works which belong
to my soul's fertility,
why don't you give your life to me?
Why should your breasts not let
my lips suck your eternity?
Perhaps sweet words, you resonate
in the same air in which my ears,
turned into dust, now oscillate,
marching in step with you!
A sparkling wake upon the sea
left by a ship submerged.
Oh fearsome mystery!
The footprints of a man since dead!

Listen to the voice that rises
from the grave to gently whisper
in your ear the secret truth:
'I no longer am, my friend'.
Again it comes to say to you:
'I no longer am my friend'.
It is my song, it is not me
which carries in this world
the shadow of my ghostly self,
of my abysmal nullity.
You hear me, reader, I do not hear
myself: a truth so trite

la dejamos caer como la lluvia,
es lluvia de tristeza,
es gota del océano
de la amargura.
¿Dónde irás a pudrirte, canto mío?
¿En qué rincón oculto
darás tu último aliento?
¡Tú también morirás, morirá todo,
y en silencio infinito
dormirá para siempre la esperanza!

that it's treated with disdain
as one might listen to the rain.
But the drops are drops of grief
come from an ocean of regret.
Where, my song, will you decay?
In what mysterious neighbourhood
will your last breath fade away?
For you will die, and all will die,
and in perpetual quietude
hope will forever dormant lie.

11 LEYENDO UN LIBRO VIVO
DE UN AMIGO MUERTO

Cuando tu libro leía
resucitar te sentí;
y tú, ¿te sentiste en mí
resucitar? Alma mía,

¿eres sólo mía?, dime.
Juntos todos ¿no vivimos
acaso en Dios? ¿Ni partimos
de una unidad que redime

de ser tú tú y yo yo?
¿Escribiste el libro, amigo,
solo o lo escribí contigo
sin saberlo? ¿O lo escribió

Dios para unirnos en gloria?
Quien lo sabe...
Todas las aves un ave
y un solo vuelo la historia.

Mientras te leo te vivo
y me vives tú, aun muerto...
¿Muerto? ¿Qué es esto? Lo cierto
que leyéndote, cautivo

de tu letra viva, agarro
espíritu, el de los dos,
y siento surgir a Dios
de nuestro mutuo barro.

11 READING THE LIVING BOOK
OF A DEAD FRIEND

When I your book was reading
I felt you were living again.
Did you gain through me your being?
Did you feel yourself return?

Tell me, my soul, do you belong
to me alone? Does everyone not lead
a common life in God? Do we
not come from one whose heed

saves you from you and me from me?
Was this book written by yourself,
my friend, or did I unknowingly write
with you? Or was it God Himself

who wrote to bring us both together
in glorious harmony? To see the light...
All birds become a single bird
and all of history a single flight.

For as I read I give you breath
as you give me breath though dead...
Dead? What do I say? The truth
is that while reading you I'm led

to grasp the spirit, yours and mine,
held in your living word, a way
to feel God's presence rising up
from our common mortal clay.

12 [A LA ESPERA]

Al pie del molino de viento
hilaba la vieja su rueca,
miraba al sendero a lo lejos,
señero del cielo a la puerta.

Pasaban las horas de arreo,
pasaban las nubes a vela,
quedaba tan sólo el sendero,
hilaba su copo la vieja.

Cruzaba un milano en el cielo,
cruzaba una hormiga por tierra,
cruzaban las horas de arreo,
miraba al sendero la vieja.

Hilaban las aspas al viento,
molía la vieja en su rueca,
llegaba la noche en silencio,
nacían en paz las estrellas;

se alzaba hasta el cielo el sendero,
estrellas calzaban sus huellas,
dormían tranquilos los muertos
hilando sus sueños en tierra.

12 **WAITING**

The old woman was spinning her thread
outside the windmill's store,
but her eyes were fixed on the lane
that stretched from the sky to the door.

The work day was moving along
as the clouds sailed away in the wind,
the old woman was spinning her skein
while only the lane stood still.

A kite traced its flight in the sky,
an ant made its way on the plain,
the working day was all but done
as the old woman watched the lane.

The sails were spinning the wind,
the woman was milling the yarn,
in silence the night stole in,
in stillness the stars were born.

The lane reached up to the sky
and the stars marked out its trail,
the dead lay peacefully asleep
spinning their dreams in the grave.

13 [RÍOS DE MI VIDA]

Nervión, Tormes, Bidasoa,
venas de sangre de peña
donde mi nave la proa
puso a la mar con que sueña.

Vuestro sino ir a la fuente
de vuestros raudales; nube
maternal, lluvia, torrente...
al bajar mi mente sube.

Agua de mi alma, verduras
espejas en el remanso;
darán flor en las honduras
cuando al fin logres descanso.

13 RIVERS OF MY LIFE

Nervión, Tormes, Bidasoa,
veins of blood through rocky streams
where my boat has set its course
towards the sea of its dreams.

Your fate points you to the source
of your richness. Downstream comes
fecund cloud and rain and flood
while my mind upriver roams.

Waters of my soul, green shoots
are reflected in your pools;
they will flourish in the depths
when you lie in quietude.

14 **IRREQUIETUM COR**

Recio Jesús ibero, el de Teresa,
tú que en la más recóndita morada
del alma mueres, cumple la promesa
que entre abrazos de fe diste a la amada.

Gozó dolor sabroso, Quijotesa
a lo divino, que dejó asentada
nuestra España inmortal cuya es la empresa:
«sólo existe lo eterno: ¡Dios o nada!»

Si Él se hizo hombre para hacernos dioses,
mortal para librarnos de la muerte,
¿qué mucho, osado corazón, que así oses

romper los grillos de la humana suerte
y que en la negra vida no reposes
bregando sin cesar por poseerte?

14 **RESTLESS HEART**

Teresa's Jesus, of tough Iberian stock,
you who dies in the innermost recesses
of the soul, come to fulfil the pledge you gave
to the bride amidst your comforting caresses.

Our lady Quixote turned divine received
a joyful pain which found its sanctuary
in our immortal Spain, whose cry became:
"eternity is all; it's God or nullity!"

If He to make us gods a man became,
accepted death to free us from mortality,
is it too much, brave heart, for you to strain

to break the shackles of our destiny
and that in this dark life you take no rest
but struggle to affirm your right to be?

15 LA ORACIÓN DEL ATEO

Oye mi ruego tú, Dios que no existes,
y en tu nada recoge estas mis quejas,
tú que a los pobres hombres nunca dejas
sin consuelo de engaño. No resistes

a nuestro ruego y nuestro anhelo vistes.
Cuanto tú de mi mente más te alejas
más recuerdo las plácidas consejas
con que mi ama endulzóme noches tristes.

¡Qué grande eres, mi Dios! Eres tan grande
que no eres sino Idea; es muy angosta
la realidad por mucho que se espande

para abarcarte. Sufro yo a tu costa,
Dios no existente, pues si Tú existieras
existiría yo también de veras.

15 THE ATHEIST'S PRAYER

Listen to my prayer, oh non-existent God,
and in your unreality receive my lamentations,
you who will not leave our hapless race alone
without the reassurance of empty self-deception.

Unyielding to our prayer, you build up our desire.
For as you move away out of my sight
the more my mind recalls the placid tales
with which my nurse lit up those anxious nights.

How great you are my God! Indeed so great
that all you are is Idea; for reality itself, though it
expands, yet stays too cramped to accommodate

your presence. I suffer pain because of you,
oh non-existent God, for if you did exist
my own existence would be assuredly true.

16 SALMO II

Fe soberbia, impía,
la que no duda,
la que encadena a Dios a nuestra idea.
«Dios te habla por mi boca»,
dicen impíos,
y sienten en su pecho:
«¡por boca de Dios te hablo!».
No te ama, oh Verdad, quien nunca duda,
quien piensa poseerte,
porque eres infinita, y en nosotros,
Verdad, no cabes.
eres, Verdad, la muerte;
muere la pobre mente al recibirte.
Eres la muerte hermosa,
eres la eterna muerte,
el descanso final, santo reposo;
en ti el pensar se duerme.
Buscando la verdad va el pensamiento,
y él no es si no la busca;
si al fin la encuentra,
se para y duerme.
La vida es duda,
y la fe sin la duda es sólo muerte.
Y es la muerte el sustento de la vida,
y de la fe la duda.
Mientras viva, Señor, la duda dame,
fe pura cuando muera;
la vida dame en vida
y en la muerte la muerte;
dame, Señor, la muerte con la vida.

16 **PSALM II**

A faith that's free from doubt
is faith impious and proud,
God chained to our idea
of Him. "God speaks through me"
the impious will declare,
but in their hearts they feel
it's they who through God speak.
He does not love you, Truth, who never doubts,
he who can only see your lasting youth
because you're not confined by finitude;
our home cannot accommodate you, Truth.
When you, oh Truth, arrive,
our minds cannot survive.
You are our death alluring,
you are our death enduring,
our minds' final retreat,
a sacred place to sleep.
Our minds set off to search for truth,
a mission that must be fulfilled;
and if at last truth is unveiled
our minds will stop, our hearts be stilled.
The blood of life is doubt,
faith without doubt is death,
and death the food of life
and doubt the food of faith.
While I'm alive, my Lord, give me my doubts
and when I die, my Lord, give me my faith.
In life my life I need,
in death I need my death;
together life and death tell me I am.

Tú eres el que eres;
si yo te conociera
dejaría de ser quien soy ahora,
y en ti me fundiría,
siendo Dios como Tú, Verdad suprema.
Dame vivir en vida,
dame morir en muerte,
dame en la fe dudar en tanto viva,
dame la pura fe luego que muera.
Lejos de mí el impío pensamiento
de tener tu verdad aquí en la vida,
pues sólo es tuyo
quien confiesa, Señor, no conocerte.
Lejos de mí, Señor, el pensamiento
de enterrarte en la idea,
la impiedad de querer con raciocinios
demostrar tu existencia.
Yo te siento, Señor, no te conozco,
tu Espíritu me envuelve,
si conozco contigo,
si eres la luz de mi conocimiento
¿cómo he de conocerte, Inconocible?
La luz por la que vemos
es invisible.
Creo, Señor, en ti, sin conocerte.
Mira que de mi espíritu los hijos
de un espíritu mudo viven presos;
libértalos, Señor, que caen rodando
en fuego y agua;
libértalos, que creo,
creo, confío en Ti, Señor; ayuda
mi desconfianza.

"I am who am" you said; you are who is.
If I could only get to see your face
I would no longer feel myself to exist.
In your being, my own would be dissolved,
I would become, like You, the Truth supreme.
In life give me my breath,
in death give me my dream,
in faith give me my doubt,
in death give me my faith.
Banish from me the impious thought
that here I could attain your truth;
for those alone you will adopt
who plead their ignorance of You.
Banish from me, my Lord, the thought
of reducing You to ideas,
of pretending that with reasons
I can prove that you are real.
Without, Lord, meeting You
your presence I can tell.
Your knowledge is inside,
your light is in myself.
How shall I recognize
what does not come in view?
I do not see the light
but I believe in You.
Enchained by one who does not speak,
see the children of my blood;
cast out the devil, Lord, and leave
them free to fall in fire and flood.
Lord set them free, for I believe.
I place my trust in You, oh Lord,
help me to quell my unbelief.

III

THE LAND

17 SALAMANCA

Alto soto de torres que al ponerse
tras las encinas que el celaje esmaltan
dora a los rayos de su lumbre el padre
    sol de Castilla;

bosque de piedras que arrancó la historia
a las entrañas de la tierra madre,
remanso de quietud, yo te bendigo,
    ¡mi Salamanca!

Miras a un lado, allende el Tormes lento,
de las encinas el follaje pardo
cual el follaje de tu piedra, inmoble,
    denso y perenne.

Y de otro lado, por la calva Armuña,
ondea el trigo, cual tu piedra, de oro,
y entre los surcos al morir la tarde
    duerme el sosiego.

Duerme el sosiego, la esperanza duerme,
de otras cosechas y otras dulces tardes
las horas al correr sobre la tierra
    dejan su rastro.

Al pie de tus sillares, Salamanca,
de las cosechas del pensar tranquilo
que año tras año maduró en tus aulas
    duerme el recuerdo.

Duerme el recuerdo, la esperanza duerme,
y es el tranquilo curso de tu vida

17 SALAMANCA

High grove of towers which, as he sets
behind the oak trees that adorn the sky,
the radiant father of Castile, our sun,
    bedecks in gold.

Forest of stones which history did wrest
from the bowels of mother earth,
haven of peace, I bless you ,
    my Salamanca!

On one side, beyond the languid Tormes,
you overlook the foliage of the dusky oaks,
which like the foliage of your stone is still,
    dense and eternal;

on the other, upon the treeless plains of Armuña,
the undulating wheat of gold, just like your stone,
and as the evening sinks into the furrowed earth
    peace sleeps.

Peace lies asleep, hope lies asleep, and as
they pass over the earth the hours leave
their trace of other harvests and other
    placid nights.

Memories of harvests of tranquil thought
which in your lecture halls yearly matured,
now at the foot of your stones, Salamanca,
    lie in repose.

Memories rest, and hope rests too,
and the serene course of your life

como el crecer de las encinas, lento,
    lento y seguro.

De entre tus piedras seculares, tumba
de remembranzas del ayer glorioso,
de entre tus piedras recogió mi espíritu
    fe, paz y fuerza.

En este patio que se cierra al mundo
y con ruinosa crestería borda
limpio celaje, al pie de la fachada
    que de plateros

ostenta filigranas en la piedra,
en este austero patio, cuando cede
el vocerío estudiantil, susurra
    voz de recuerdos.

    [...]

¡Oh, Salamanca!, entre tus piedras de oro
aprendieron a amar los estudiantes
mientras los campos que te ciñen daban
    jugosos frutos.

Del corazón en las honduras guardo
tu alma robusta; cuando yo me muera,
guarda, dorada Salamanca mía,
    tú mi recuerdo.

Y cuando el sol al acostarse encienda
el oro secular que te recama,
con tu lenguaje, de lo eterno heraldo,
    di tú que he sido.

is like the oak trees slow of growth,
  sure and slow.

From your age-old stones, a graveyard
of remembrances of an illustrious past,
from those stones my spirit gathered faith,
  peace and strength.

In this cloister shuttered to the world,
and with a crumbling crest that borders
a pure sky, at the foot of the façade
  which shows

the filigrees of silversmiths on stone,
in this forbidding cloister one can hear,
when the clamour of students fades away,
  murmurs of the past.

  […]

Oh, Salamanca!, amidst your stones of gold
the students learnt to love, whilst
in the embracing fields the fruit
  was turning ripe.

In the depths of my heart your noble soul
I keep; and when I reach my end,
oh golden Salamanca, be sure you keep
  a memory of me.

And when the sun goes down and lights
the timeless gold that is your garb,
with your voice, a herald of eternity,
  say that I lived.

18 [TIERRA DEL TORMES]

Agua del Tormes, nieve de Gredos,
sal de mi tierra, sol de mi cielo,
pan de la Armuña mollar y prieto,
leche de cabra del llano escueto,
puestas de soles de rosa eterno,
sombra de encina que espeja el Puerto,
cantos de charros, todo recuerdos;
la carretera de mis paseos
de lazarillo, soñaba el ciego,
balcón de estío, ¡ay mis vencejos!
Catedral Vieja, queda lo eterno,
Santo Domingo, reposo inquieto,
Arco de Lapa, fervor obrero;
bancos del aula de mis ensueños;
noches de casa junto al brasero,
duermen los míos, canta el sereno;
siglos de vida que se me fueron.

18 LAND OF THE TORMES

Waters of Tormes, snows of Gredos,
sun of my sky, salt of my clay,
bread from Armuña brown and soft,
milk of the goats from the frugal plain,
shadows of oak on the mountain pass,
tinted sunsets of heavenly rose,
countryfolk songs recalling days past,
the walks I took along the road,
where the guide-boy led, the blind man dreamed,
balconies in summer where nested the swifts,
convent of St Dominic, anxious retreat,
the Old Cathedral, a perduring gift,
Arch of La Lapa, the labourer's mission,
benches in the classroom of my expositions,
nights spent at home next to the fire,
the watchman calling, my children sleeping,
years of my life forever receding.

19 AL TORMES

Desde Gredos, espalda de Castilla,
rodando, Tormes, sobre tu dehesa
pasas brezando el sueño de Teresa
junto a Alba la ducal dormida villa.

De la Flecha gozándote en la orilla
un punto te detienes en la presa
que el soto de Fray Luis cantando besa
y con tu canto animas al que trilla.

De Salamanca cristalino espejo
retratas luego sus doradas torres,
pasas solemne bajo el puente viejo

de los romanos y el hortal recorres
que Meléndez cantara. Tu consejo
no de mi pecho, Tormes mío, borres.

19 TO THE RIVER TORMES

From Gredos, the backbone of Castile,
oh Tormes, you roll across your pastures,
cradling St Teresa in her raptures,
and pass through ducal Alba, sleepy ville.

On the banks of La Flecha you stay still,
stopping for a moment in the dam
that kisses with a song Fray Luis's farm,
and hearten the thresher in the field.

Neath the old Roman bridge you pass with pride
to mirror Salamanca's towers of gold
with crystal clarity, and on you glide

towards that fruit-laden fertile part
that Meléndez eulogized. Oh Tormes,
do not remove your wisdom from my heart.

20 LA PEÑA DE FRANCIA

Madre Blanca de Castilla,
que a Francia le dio un rey santo;
maternidad castellana
de corazón todo blanco.

Nuestra Señora la Virgen,
Madre de Dios soberano,
la de la Peña de Francia
en el corazón serrano

de España, sobre las Hurdes,
de Extremadura barranco;
maternidad castellana,
que está de piedad sangrando.

Peña de Francia desnuda,
¡ay corazón descarnado!,
Madre Blanca de Castilla
dióle a Francia Luis el Santo.

20 THE ROCK OF FRANCE

Blanche of Castile, the mother
– Castilian maternity –
who gave France a saintly king,
had a heart of piety.

Our Lady is the Virgin
Mother of God sovereign,
Virgin of the Rock of France
in the heart of highland Spain

above the lands of Las Hurdes
and the Extremaduran range,
a Castilian motherhood,
bleeds for us with deep concern.

A naked Rock of France,
her heart laid bare with pain,
Blanche of Castile our mother
gave France King Louis the saint.

21 [EL LAGO DE SAN MARTÍN]

San Martín de Castañeda,
espejo de soledades,
el lago recoge edades
de antes del hombre y se queda

soñando en la santa calma
del cielo de las alturas,
la que se sume en honduras
de anegarse, ¡pobre!, el alma.

Men Rodríguez, aguilucho
de Sanabria, el ala rota,
ya el cotarro no alborota
para cobrarse el conducho.

Campanario sumergido
de Valverde de Lucerna,
toque de agonía eterna
bajo el agua del olvido.

La historia paró; al sendero
de San Bernardo la vida
retorna, y todo se olvida,
lo que no ha sido primero.

21 THE LAKE AT SAN MARTIN

The lake at San Martín
existed all alone
before the time of man,
and yet it still dreams on

in the seraphic peace
of the heaven above,
which plunges in the depths
of a spirit in flood.

Of Sanabria petty lord,
Men Rodríguez lost his claim
and agitates no more
to seize his vassals' grain.

Submerged within the lake
Valverde's belfry chimes
an eternal agony
under the waters of time.

History stands still and life
to St Bernard's trail withdraws;
oblivion threatens all,
and first what never was.

22 [MEDINA DE RIOSECO]

Medina de Rioseco,
varadas tus cuatro naves
de páramo en que las aves
tejen nido, guardan eco

de los siglos de la tierra
seca y dura, castellana,
la del eterno mañana,
que en resignación se encierra.

Rubio mar, te ciñe el trigo,
y el polvo que fue tu gente
da a la que te es de presente
contra el hambre escaso abrigo.

Hunde, Medina, su cuño
sobre ti en redondo el cielo,
y hunden tus naves su vuelo
en mar seco, tu terruño.

22 MEDINA DE RIOSECO

Medina de Rioseco,
your four ships which sailed the moors,
and which house your nesting birds,
now aground echo the lure

of past ages on your lands
dry and rocky, like Castile,
land of future expectations
resigned to its present ills.

Golden seas of wheat surround you,
but the dust of generations
barely feeds the hungry mouths
of your present population.

The sky, Medina, leaves its stamp
upon the surrounding plain,
as your ships incline their bows
in the dry sea of your terrain.

23 LA VOZ DE LA CAMPANA

Cuando del mar del sueño entre las nieblas
cual puerto un día nuevo surge al alba,
cae desde el cielo matinal el canto
    de la campana.

Es voz del pueblo en cuyo seno vivo,
sus miles de almas dan una palabra
que ni pide, ni niega, ni se queja:
    tan sólo canta.

En el silencio del señor se pierde
y Dios en su silencio nos la guarda,
voz que ni da, ni pide, ni se queja:
    voz de esperanza.

La voz del ángel es, del mensajero
que a Dios eleva de mi pueblo el alma;
nada le pide, ni le da, ni niega:
    tan sólo canta.

Canta el arcano de la pobre vida,
canta el misterio que la voz embarga,
y a las tristezas que la noche incuba
    presta sus alas.

Lengua de bronce tiene el alma ruda
de este mi pueblo, y al rayar el alba
hace ya siglos que su voz suspira
    divinas ansias.

23 THE VOICE OF THE BELL

A new day emerges from the sea of dreams,
like a haven surging through the mists of dawn,
and from the morning sky there come the chimes
    of bells.

The voice of the people in whose midst I stay;
they nothing request, nor deny, nor lament;
thousands of souls with but one word to say:
    their song.

The voice of my people is lost in the Lord,
and God in his silence grants it his abode;
their voice demands nothing but sings to record
    their hope.

An angel's voice it is, messenger divine
come to elevate my people's soul to God,
no plea, no denial, no gift to begrime
    their hymn.

It sings private secrets of their life's concerns,
it sings of mysteries that command a song,
and to the sorrows brought by the night it lends
    its wings.

The rugged soul of the people of these plains
has a tongue of bronze, and at the break of morn
for centuries its voice has sung in godly strains
    its dreams.

24 **PORTUGAL (i)**

Portugal, Portugal, tierra descalza,
acurrucada junto al mar, tu madre,
llorando soledades
de trágicos amores,
mientras tus pies desnudos las espumas
saladas bañan,
tu verde cabellera suelta al viento
–cabellera de pinos rumorosos–
los codos descansando en las rodillas,
y la cara morena entre ambas palmas,
clavas tus ojos donde el sol se acuesta
solo en la mar inmensa,
y en el lento naufragio así meditas
de tus glorias de Oriente,
cantando fados quejumbrosa y lenta.

24 **PORTUGAL (i)**

Portugal, Portugal, barefoot land,
curled up against your mother
the sea, you come to grieve
your tragic loves while you permit
the salty foam
to bathe your naked feet.
Your verdant hair blowing in the breeze
– tresses of rustling pines –
with elbows resting on your knees,
with tanned face resting on your hands,
you fix your eyes far out to sea
where all alone the sun descends,
and in that unhurried wane
you dream your glories of the East
singing fados in wistful vein.

25 **PORTUGAL (ii)**

Del atlántico mar en las orillas
desgreñada y descalza una matrona
se sienta al pie de sierra que corona
triste pinar. Apoya en las rodillas

los codos y en las manos las mejillas,
y clava ansiosos ojos de leona
en la puesta del sol; el mar entona
su trágico cantar de maravillas.

Dice de luengas tierras y de azares
mientras ella sus pies en las espumas
bañando sueña en el fatal imperio

que se le hundió en los tenebrosos mares
y mira cómo entre agoreras brumas
se alza Don Sebastián, rey del misterio.

25 PORTUGAL (ii)

Upon a ridge of sombre pines
high above the Atlantic seas
a barefoot unkempt maiden sits.
Resting her elbows on her knees,

her face held in her hands,
she turns her feline anxious eyes
towards the setting sun; the sea
bemoans its tales of enterprise

and tells of fates in distant lands,
while, dipping her feet into the waves,
the maiden dreams of empires sunk

in murky seas and turns her gaze
where Don Sebastian, mystic King,
rises from the prophetic haze.

IV

EXILE

26 [MI OTRO SINO]

Al frisar los sesenta, mi otro sino,
el que dejé al dejar mi natal villa,
brota del fondo del ensueño y brilla
un nuevo porvenir en mi camino.

Vuelve el que pudo ser y que el destino
sofocó en una cátedra en Castilla;
me llega por la mar hasta esta orilla
trayendo nueva rueca y nuevo lino.

Hacerme, al fin, el que soñé, poeta,
vivir mi ensueño del caudillo fuerte
que el fugitivo azar prende y sujeta;

volver las tornas, dominar la suerte,
y en la vida de obrar, por fuera inquieta,
derretir el espanto de la muerte.

26 MY OTHER FATE

As I reach sixty, my other destiny,
that which lay forgotten in my native town,
springs from the depths of dreams and shines a light
upon new ventures along my earthly round.

The one returns whom fate decreed should be
displaced by the professor in Castile;
upon these distant shores he arrives by sea
bringing new flax to spin on a new wheel.

To turn myself at last into the poet I dreamt,
to live my distant hope of overlord supreme
who grips a fleeting chance and holds it firm;

to turn the tables, to command my fate,
and in ceaseless action restive to the eye,
the fear of death to crush and dissipate.

27 [OLAS LEJANAS]

¿Cual de vosotras, olas de consuelo
que rodando venís desde la raya
celestial y surcando con la laya
espumosa a la mar el leve suelo,

cuál de vosotras que aviváis mi anhelo
viene del fiero golfo de Vizcaya?
¿Cual de vosotras con su lengua ensaya
cantos que fueron mi primer desvelo?

¿Sois acaso sirenas o delfines,
a brizar mi recuerdo estremecido
que de la mar se ahoga en los confines?

¿Cual de vosotras, olas del olvido,
trae acá los zortzicos danzarines
de los regatos de mi dulce nido?

27 **DISTANT WAVES**

Which one of you, consoling waves who roll
towards these shores from the horizon's line
while furrowing the surface of the sea
and planting it with foaming crests of brine,

which one of you, waves who rouse my yearnings,
has travelled from the stormy sea of Biscay?
Which one of you with your own voice intones
songs which were my wakening of early days?

Are you sirens or dolphins come maybe
to cradle my convulsive memories
which founder in the confines of the sea?

Which one of you, oh waves of vanished days,
is bringing to me those pulsating tunes
that fed the dreams of childhood hideaways?

28 **BETANCURIA**

Enjalbegada tumba es Betancuria,
donde la vida como acaba empieza,
tránsito lento a que el mortal se aveza
lejos del tiempo y de su cruel injuria.

Se oye en esta barranca la canturria
de la resignación en la pobreza,
la majorera–blancas tocas–reza
entre ruinas, soledad, penuria...

Desnuda la montaña en que el camello
buscando entre las piedras flor de aulaga
marca en el cielo su abatido cuello;

mas de la tierra en la sedienta llaga
pone el geráneo con su flor el sello
de la mujer que nuestra pena apaga.

28 **BETANCURIA**

Betancuria is a whitewashed grave
where life comes to an end as it commenced,
a gentle passage to which man adapts
far from the madding crowd and its offence.

Across the gully can be heard a chant
that sings of life in poverty unrelieved;
a local woman, white toque on her head,
prays amidst ruins, emptiness, and need.

Searching for gorse among the adamant,
a camel on the naked mountain makes
a silhouette against the firmament;

but on the dryness of the flinty slope
the flower of a geranium celebrates
the woman's fervour to restore our hope.

29 [FUERTEVENTURA]

Raíces como tú en el Oceano,
echó mi alma ya, Fuerteventura,
de la cruel historia la amargura
me quitó cual si fuese con la mano.

Toqué a su toque el insondable arcano
que es la fuente de nuestra desventura,
y en sus olas la mágica escritura
descifré del más alto Soberano.

Un oasis me fuiste, isla bendita;
la civilización es un desierto
donde la fe con la verdad se irrita;

cuando llegué a tu roca llegué a puerto,
y esperándome allí a la última cita
sobre tu mar vi el cielo todo abierto.

29 FUERTEVENTURA

Fuerteventura, just like you, my soul
has put down roots deep in the Ocean sea,
which took away as if with its own hands
the bitterness of a cruel history.

Its touch conveyed the awesome mystery
which is the source of our anxiety,
and in its waves I learnt the magic script
of He who holds supreme authority.

Oh blessed isle, you were my sanctuary.
Civilization is a desert land
where faith in reason meets her adversary.

Upon your rock a haven did I find,
and for my final rendezvous, the skies
above your seas offered a welcome sign.

30 [EN EL EXILIO]

Super flumina Babylonis.

Es el destierro mi tierra,
donde llueve manso orvallo
sin duro sol de justicia
en la mocedad del año.

Es el destierro mi patria,
junto a la mar que cantando
va la verdad escondida,
sin palabras, sin engaños.

De un sauce de la frontera
he recogido estos cantos;
dormían en su follaje,
briza de la mar brizábalos,

junto a este río que corta
como una daga a lo largo
el corazón de Vasconia,
mi tierra de mayorazgo.

Es el destierro mi tierra
donde llueve manso orvallo
sin duro sol de justicia
en la mocedad del año.

30 **IN EXILE**

On the rivers of Babylon

My exile is my native land,
where soft rain gives no fear
without the harsh sun to chasten
the young days of the year.

My exile is my fatherland
next to the humming sea,
whose song without words cantillates
the truth without deceit.

From a willow on the frontier
I picked these melodies;
among its leaves they were asleep
rocked by the heaving seas,

beside the river that dissects,
as if a knife had carved,
the heart of that Basque fatherland
which I inherited.

My exile is my native land,
where soft rain gives no fear
without the harsh sun to chasten
the young days of the year.

31 [ROMANCES FRONTERIZOS]

Ay romances fronterizos
que fraguaron la leyenda
de la reconquista patria,
dadme el soplo de entereza
que ha llevado vuestro vuelo
sobre las benditas tierras
que el Duero y el Tajo hermanos
con aguas de Gredos riegan.

Ay romances fronterizos,
resonantes de las guerras
entre moros y cristianos,
regaladme la grandeza
de vuestra voz entrañada
para que cante mi guerra,
la que encinta mis recuerdos
al amor de la frontera.

Que de Altobiscar el canto
se oiga en mis cantos de guerra
de mi íntima reconquista,
la que hace de mi alma tierra
donde los hijos de España
vivan por siempre, y que sean
mis romances fronterizos
pedestal de mi leyenda.

31 **FRONTIER BALLADS**

Oh ballads of the frontier,
forged out of the legendary
reconquest of our homeland,
grant me a breath of that energy
which has taken you in flight
over those exalted plains
enriched by brothers Douro and Tagus
with waters from the Gredos range.

Oh ballads of the frontier,
resonant of ancient warfare
between the Christians and Moors,
grant me the majestic power
of your heartfelt recitation
so that I can sing my war,
war that bonds my recollections
to the love of the frontier.

Let Altobiscar resound
with the war cry of my songs
of an intimate reconquest,
that which makes of my own soul
a land in which the sons of Spain
will live forever, thus making
my ballads of the frontier
the foundation of my legend.

32 **ORHOIT GUTAZ**

Pasasteis como pasan por el roble
las hojas que arrebata en primavera
pedrisco intempestivo;
pasasteis, hijos de mi raza noble,
vestida el alma de infantil eusquera,
pasasteis al archivo
de mármol funeral de una iglesiuca
que en el regazo recogido y verde
del Pirineo vasco
al tibio sol del monte se acurruca.
Abajo el Bidasoa va y se pierde
en la mar; un peñasco
recoge de sus olas el gemido,
que pasan, tal las hojas rumorosas,
tal vosotros, oscuros
hijos sumisos del hogar henchido
de silenciosa tradición. Las fosas
que a vuestros huesos, puros,
blancos, les dan de última cuna lecho,
fosas que abrió el cañón en sorda guerra,
no escucharán el canto
de la materna lluvia que el helecho
deja caer en vuestra patria tierra
como celeste llanto...
No escucharán la esquila de la vaca
que en la ladera, al pie del caserío,
dobla su cuello al suelo,
ni a lo lejos la voz de la resaca
de la mar que amamanta a vuestro río

32 REMEMBER US

You passed through life as through an oak
pass young spring leaves plucked out
by an untimely hailstorm from the tree;
you passed, sons of my noble race,
your souls draped in a boyish Basque tongue,
into the marble registers
of death of a chapel nestling,
midst greenery and tepid sun,
in the secluded sanctuary
of a Basque Pyrenean hill.
The river Bidasoa below
goes to the sea to meet its end;
a rock records the moaning sound
left by its waves that pass like those
whispering leaves of spring, like you,
unknown, submissive sons from homes
suffused with silent history.
The graves which gave a resting place
to your bones so pure and white,
graves which cannon fire dug out
in heedless war, will not perceive
the song of fertile rain which drips
from ferns upon your fatherland
like a celestial lamentation.
They will not hear upon the hill,
next to the countryhouse, the bells
of cows reaching the ground to feed;
nor distant sounds of undertows
in the sea that sucks your river

y es canto de consuelo.
Fuisteis como corderos, en los ojos
guardando la sonrisa dolorida
–lágrimas del ocaso–
de vuestras madres – el alma de hinojos –
y en la agonía de la paz la vida
rendisteis al acaso...
¿Por qué?, ¿por qué? Jamás esta pregunta
terrible torturó vuestra inocencia;
nacisteis..., nadie sabe
por qué ni para qué...; ara la yunta
y el campo que ara es toda su conciencia
y canta y vuela el ave...
¡Oroit gutaz! Pedís nuestro recuerdo,
y una lección nos dais de mansedumbre;
calle el porqué..., vivamos
como habéis muerto, sin porqué, es lo cuerdo;
los ríos a la mar..., es la costumbre
y con ella pasamos.

and which sings of consolation.
Like lambs you went, and in your eyes
you took with you sorrowful smiles
– laced with tears for a sun that sets –
of mothers with their souls prostrate,
and in the mortal cause of peace
you sacrificed your lives to chance.
Why, oh why? Never did the dreaded
question torture your innocent
souls; you were born and no-one knows
reason or purpose... The oxen plough
the field and that is what they know;
the bird knows how to sing and fly...
Remember us! That's what you ask
and offer us a lesson in
assent. Let us forget the why,
and let us live like you have died.
That's sense; the river to the sea
and we to our banalities.

33 EL CEMENTERIO DE HENDAYA

Tañe la mar con quejumbrosa brisa
tus cipreses, pendiente camposanto;
pone el sol entre nubes su sonrisa
     sobre tu manto.

Tus mármoles son cresta de las olas
que se fijaron en su inmoble espuma;
bajo ellas duerme su reposo a solas,
     –¡tristor rezuma!–

la gente que pasó, náufraga errante
del paraíso de antes de la vida;
guarda los siglos en un sólo instante,
     todo lo olvida.

Cuando a tus plantas sube la marea,
te ofrece espejo palpitante; baja,
y el fango es otro espejo y se recrea
     con tu escurraja.

Con rayos que hila de su triste entraña
flotante velo de antes de la cuna,
en ti en las noches una telaraña
     teje la luna.

El Bidasoa su agua dulce meje
con la amargura de la mar materna,
hundiéndose en su abismo que protege
     de la galerna.

El barrio bajo por ventanas mira
de su recinto las cerradas hueses;
cuando al caer la noche se retira,
     sus mentes presas

33 THE CEMETERY AT HENDAYE

A plaintive breeze come from the sea
plucks a cypress on your sacred slope;
between the clouds the sun's smile falls
    upon your robe.

Headstones like crests of waves congeal
in an immobile sea of foam;
beneath them take their rest alone
    – oh piteous home! –

the souls who walked this earthly life
after exile from paradise;
their history, reduced to stone,
    forgotten lies.

The high tide laps your feet and holds
a trembling mirror to your face,
and when it ebbs the mirror sweeps
    away your waste.

Like floating film from mists of time,
the moon extrudes its thread at night
to spin around you with its rays
    a web of light.

With bitter brine from mother sea
the fresh Bidasoa waters mix
as they seek refuge from the storm
    in the abyss.

The lower quarter of the town
that overlooks your shuttered graves,
when nightfall comes and it withdraws,
    seeking escape

de la fatiga del vivir, repasa
de tu heredad la tierra solariega
y se siente al amparo de la casa
    y a ella se pliega.

Yace aquí el pueblo que pasó y se queda
mejido al barro que le da sustento;
la historia en tanto por el mundo rueda,
    la lleva el viento.

from life's exhausting toil, it sees
the ancient soils of your estate
and contemplates the welcome shield
    of its embrace.

Here lie a people gone yet stayed
in clay that gives them nourishment,
and meanwhile history flies past
    indifferent.

V

LANGUAGE AND POETRY

34 [LAS CARAS DE LA POESÍA]

¡Qué de caras la verdad!
Qué infinito mi universo
de palabras que en el verso
– espejo de humanidad –

lucho a encerrar por si acaso
se perdiese alguna cara...
Mano de Dios ¡tan avara!
¿De Dios? Más bien del Acaso.

Acaso, sellada fuente
de la rima y del estilo,
cárcel y a la vez asilo
de libertad inconsciente;

pozo de contradicción
donde el si y el no acoplados
dan a luz, resucitados,
a dar vida a la canción.

34 THE FACES OF POETRY

So many faces make up truth!
And stretching to infinity
so many words make up my verse
– mirror of humanity –

in which I strive to encapsulate
every face lest one were snubbed...
The hand of God is miserly.
Is it God's hand or Fortune's rub?

Fortune, a sealed fountainhead
of rhyme and style in poetry,
prison and yet refuge too
of my unconscious liberty;

a well of verbal contraries
where yes and no in harmony
come together to conceive
and give birth to melody.

35 [LA LABOR DEL POETA]

A ver, ¿qué tienes que decirte? Aguarda,
el ritmo mismo te traerá la idea
– duerme en el seno del lenguaje mudo –
busca tan sólo las palabras, ellas
te crearon el alma y al creártela
te hicieron creador; esto es poeta.

La canción vuela en busca de unas alas
que en el aire y el vuelo la sostengan,
alma sin cuerpo que suspira ansiosa
y se incorpora en carne de la letra.

Y la letra a su vez nace del vuelo
de la canción a la que ansiosa espera,
cuerpo sin alma – es un decir tan sólo
como el de alma sin cuerpo – pues que sueñan.

¿Hace el vuelo las alas o las alas
hacen el vuelo? ¡La cuestión eterna!
Cuestión de que el lenguaje filosofe,
con la filosofía se haga lengua,
y la lengua badajo que le arranque
al corazón su grito de protesta.

Protesta que es saludo y amenaza,
súplica, rezo, insulto, adiós y queja;
queja que es a su vez una pregunta
que se duele de no encontrar respuesta.
Y déjalo, que seguirás mañana,
en un mañana que aunque pasa queda...

35 THE TASK OF THE POET

Let's see what to yourself you have to say.
Wait for the rhythm to provide the idea
– it sleeps in the bosom of a silent tongue –
search only for the words, for they your soul
begat, and in this process of creation
they made you a creator, which means poet.

The melody takes off in search of wings
that will keep it aloft and aid its flight,
a disembodied soul fretfully seeking
its incarnation in the flesh of words.

Lyrics which in turn are born in the soaring
of the song which it anxiously awaits;
a soulless body – like disembodied soul
a mere expression, for they build on dreams.

Does the flight beget the wings? Do the wings
beget the flight? Eternal question mark!
For is it language that begets the idea
or is it the idea that begets language,
and language the clapper of the bell that wrings
the peal of protest from the beating heart?

A protest which is greeting, threat, appeal,
insult, prayer, adieu and inculpation,
but also one might say interrogation
which goes without response and feels aggrieved.
But let it be; tomorrow you'll restart
in a tomorrow which will fly yet last.

36 [LA PALABRA QUE VIBRA]

La vibración de mi mano
no sólo la espada lleva,
la lleva al salir de mi honda
temblando de ardor la piedra.

Va en la palabra caliente,
alma de sangre de lengua,
y en el escrito acerado,
alma de sangre de diestra.

36 THE VIBRANT WORD

The vibration of my hand
not only in the sword can ring,
but in the quivering heat
of the stone thrust from my sling.

It travels in ardent words,
life-sustaining blood of tongues,
and in scripts of tempered steel,
living blood of my right hand.

37 [LA PALABRA CRUEL]

La palabra me tortura
y no hay cura;
el postrer surco me labra
la palabra,

y de fe me da al abrigo
mi trastrigo,
la palabra, recia reja
de mi queja.

37 **THE CRUEL WORD**

Torture is the word
and treatment there is none;
the word will always plough
the final trench,

and feigning to be true
will give me chaff for wheat;
the word is the iron grille
of my lament.

38　[LA PALABRA SÍMBOLO]

La palabra es la figura
del concepto creador,
y de toda la que brota
– al salir saliendo pura –

de la boca del Señor
vive el alma, y no se agota
la fuente de la ventura;
la palabra es el amor.

Hay que figurarse el mundo
para creerlo verdad;
la figura es el profundo
sello de la eternidad.

38 THE WORD AS SYMBOL

The word is the figuration
of a creative engagement.
Out of every word that comes
– that comes free from all defacement –

from the mouth of the good Lord
the soul lives, without despoiling
the source of such felicity;
for the word is love's unveiling.

If the world is to be true
we must conceive its reality;
the symbol is the surest sign
of the seal of immortality.

39 NON OMNIS MORIAR!

Odi profanum vulgum
Horacio

«¡No todo moriré!» Así nos dice
henchido de sí mismo aquel poeta
que odia al vulgo profano y que le reta
a olvidarle esperando le eternice

el reto mismo; es calculada treta
para mejor domarle y que bautice
su gloria. Mas se escapa al infelice
que aun quien al cabo su licor enceta

jamás lo apura. Y le llegó su hora
y consagrado fue; su poesía
en nuestras mentes vive aún sonora...

Vive..., esto es se gasta. ¡No sabía,
creyendo entrar en la eternal aurora,
que hasta los muertos morirán un día!

39 NOT ALL OF ME WILL DIE!

I despise the common herd
Horace

'Not all of me will die' the poet sings
full of his own importance and disdain
for the common man, and issuing
a challenge of oblivion to sustain

that very claim; a calculated ruse
to make him co-operate and thus enshrine
his fame. But this unhappy poet forgets
that for the drinker the last drop of wine

stays in the cup. And now his time has come,
and in the hall of fame he has his place.
His verses on our tongues with life resound...

with life..., but that must bring a sure decay.
His wish for an eternal dawn evades
the truth that e'en the dead will die one day.

40 [EL NOMBRE DEL HOMBRE]

¿Qué es el Hombre? Nombre,
más que palabra.
Jacob al ángel: «¡Dime tu nombre!»
No: «¡Dame tu palabra!»
Misterio de mi nombre: ¡Miguel!
«¿Quién como Dios?»
Misterio de Dios: ¿Él?
Él no, sino Tú.
Tú son ya dos:
Él y yo.
Y ésta es toda la luz.

40 THE NAME OF MAN

What is a Man? He is a Name
more than a Word.
For Jacob to the angel said:
'tell me your name'.
He did not say 'give me your word'.
Michael my name
is mystery: 'No one like God'.
His mystery.
But is he He, or is he Thou?
For Thou is two.
He and I. That's all we see.

41 [LOS HIJOS DE SILENCIO]

Pobre Miguel, tus hijos de silencio,
aquellos en que diste tus entrañas
van en silencio y solos
pasando por delante de las casas
mas sin entrar en ellas,
pues los miran pasar como si fuesen
mendigos que molestan, no los llaman;
y aquellos adoptivos, de bullanga,
sin padre conocido,
aquellos que arrancados a la masa
les prestaste tu nombre,
estos son con aplauso y algazara
recibidos, son estos
los que tu nombre llevan, traen y exaltan.
¡Como ha de ser!, son suyos,
de los que así los miman, de su raza,
en ellos reconocen algo propio,
los engendraron ellos mismos. Nada
debe, pues, extrañarte los festejen;
son sus padres. Aguarda
para tus propios hijos mejor tiempo,
déjalos al mañana.
Las ideas expósitas hoy triunfan,
ellas llevan tu fama;
obra de caridad fue darles nombre,
¡buen provecho les haga!
Pero tus pobres hijos de silencio,
los propios de tu alma,
los de limpio linaje y noble alcurnia,

41 **THE CHILDREN OF SILENCE**

Your silent offspring, poor Miguel,
those to whom you gave your heart,
go forth unsung and all alone
past many dwellings on their march,
but no-one dares to call them in
for they are seen with wary eyes
as a scourge of mendicants.
Yet those adoptive noisy ones
of undetermined parentage,
waifs that from the heap you plucked
and to whom you lent your name,
are received with jubilation,
and acclaim; for it is they who
bring you fame and adoration.
So it was bound to be. They are
the people's own, their lineage and
their race; in them they see themselves,
for they engendered them. Marvel
not at their wild exuberance:
they are their genitors. Your own
progeny await a better chance,
their day will come tomorrow.
Today belongs to borrowed thoughts
and they disseminate your fame.
It was an act of charity
to anoint them with your name.
May they prosper and succeed.
But those poor children of your soul,
those of pure and noble strain,

los que eran tu esperanza,
ay, Miguel, mírales que van perdidos,
¿que será que les falta?
Pero no, déjalos; cuando los otros,
los expósitos vuelvan a la masa,
los tuyos surgirán limpios y enteros,
¡ellos solos se bastan!

those on whom you placed your hopes,
wander lost and shunned, Miguel.
Why are they met with such disdain?
But let them be. The changeling's face
will disappear into the crowd,
and then your pure and wholesome sons
will rise and claim their rightful place.

VI

PHILOSOPHICAL MEDITATIONS

42 [KANT Y LA RANA]

Cerré el libro que hablaba
de esencias, de existencias, de sustancias,
de accidentes y modos,
de causas y de efectos,
de materia y de forma,
de conceptos e ideas,
de noúmenos, fenómenos,
cosas en sí y en otras, opiniones,
hipótesis, teorías...,
cerré el libro y abrióse
a mis ojos el mundo.
Traspuesto había el sol ya la colina;
en el cielo esmaltábanse los álamos
y nacían entre ellos las estrellas;
la luna enjalbegaba el firmamento
cuyo fulgor difuso
en las aguas del río se bañaba.
Y, mirando a la luna, a la colina,
las estrellas, los álamos,
el río y el fulgor del firmamento,
sentí la gran mentira
de esencias, de existencias, de sustancias,
de accidentes y modos,
de causas y de efectos,
de materia y de forma,
de conceptos e ideas,
de noúmenos, fenómenos,
cosas en sí y en otras, opiniones,
hipótesis, teorías,

42 KANT AND THE FROG

I shut the book that spoke
of essences, existences and substances,
of accidents and modes,
of causes and effects,
of matter and of form,
of concepts and ideas,
of noumena, phenomena,
things in themselves and inherent in others,
opinions, hypotheses and theories...,
I shut the book and saw the world
revealed before my eyes.
The sun had set behind the hill;
against the sky the poplar trees
bedecked themselves with nascent stars;
the moon whitewashed the heavens,
whose all-pervasive glow
bathed in the waters of the river.
And looking at the moon, the hill,
the stars, the poplars,
the river and the glowing sky,
I felt the massive lie
of essences, existences and substances,
of accidents and modes,
of causes and effects,
of matter and of form,
of concepts and ideas,
of noumena, phenomena,
things in themselves and inherent in others,
opinions, hypotheses and theories,

esto es: palabras.
Sobre el libro cerrado
que yacía en la yerba,
por la luna su pasta iluminada
mas su interior a oscuras,
descansaba una rana
que iba rondando su nocturna ronda.
¡Oh Kant, cuánto te admiro!

that is to say, of words.
Upon the book now shut
which lay upon the grass,
its cover lit by moonlight
but its pages in the dark,
there sat a frog taking a rest
from its nocturnal rounds.
Oh Kant, how I admire you!

43 [¿LIBRES?]

¿Libre albedrío?
Es como el río
que se hace el cauce
y el pie del sauce
llega a besar;
en el remanso
no halla descanso;
cuanto más fluye
más se concluye;
para en la mar.

43 ARE WE FREE?

Freedom of the will?
It is like the stream
that carves its course
and kisses the feet
of the willow tree.
Even in the pools
it finds no rest;
the more it flows
the faster it goes
to die in the sea.

44 [DIOS Y LA PALABRA]

Éxodo, 33.20

Muere quien ve a Dios el rostro,
no el que oye voz de su boca
sin verle; la fe en la roca
de la palabra; me postro

ojos en tierra, el oído
al cielo, y espero el son
que entra al ciego corazón
que lo toma estremecido.

Visiones son ilusiones;
palabras son realidades;
el pasar de las edades
es cosechar oraciones.

El espíritu es aliento;
de la vida eterna norma;
la materia sólo forma
en el aire, sin cimiento.

Quien ve a Dios los ojos muere
y vive el que oye su voz
en tinieblas, desde la hoz
del abismo en que estuviere.

44 GOD AND THE WORD

Exodus, 33.20

He who sees God's face will die;
but not he who hears God's word.
Faith is based upon the rock
of the word. I look at earth

whilst I listen to the sky
and await the rhapsody
which my sightless heart will take
into fearful custody.

Words give us realities,
and our eyes hallucinations,
and the transit of past ages
is a store of recitations.

Spirit is our living breath,
standard of eternity,
matter is appearances,
air without solidity.

He who sees God's face will die,
but he who listens to His voice
reaching through the dark abyss
in life forever will rejoice.

45 **ENTROPÍA**

¿Y si el tiempo mismo
un punto parase
preso en el abismo
de la eternidad?
¿Si Dios se durmiera
y su dedo horario
marcase en la esfera
la última verdad?
¿Si contra costumbre
tornase el torrente
al hielo, a la cumbre
de donde salió?
¡Infinito enjullo
del telar divino,
cerrado capullo,
árbol, fruto y flor!

45 ENTROPY

What if time itself
for a moment stopped
trapped on the edge
of eternity?
What if God Himself
were to fall asleep,
his hand on the dial
of finality?
If the stream flowed back
to those icy peaks
defying what we know
of gravity?
The bud and the flower,
the tree and the fruit,
an eternal weave
of divinity.

46 [LAS AGUJAS DEL RELOJ]

Sí que anda tu reloj, pero es
como si no anduviera,
porque horario y minutero
se le fueron de la esfera.

Un alma desencarnada
se pierde en la eternidad,
y en un alma descarnada
no cabe la libertad.

46 THE HANDS OF THE CLOCK

Yes, your clock is working but
of working it leaves no trace
because hour and minute hands
have disappeared from its face.

A soul without its body
is lost in eternity,
for a disembodied soul
has no place for liberty.

47 FILOSOFEMAS

Decir de nuevo lo que ya se dijo,
y es nuevo el sol en cada viejo día;
nace la raya sobre un punto fijo
y sobre él muere, como tú, alma mía.
Vas tejiendo con siglos el minuto,
le haces eterno y como eterno queda;
toda la savia en un ahora –fruto–
se cuaja y fija la celeste rueda.
La vida es toda un redivivo luego;
tan sólo lo que pasa sólo dura;
el juego del pasar es todo el juego
y el poso que de Dios fragua la hondura.
'¿Qué hay, maestro, de nuevo?' El pobre sastre
remendón, sin mirar: '¿nuevo? ¡Ni el hilo...!'
Harapos son la historia y su desastre,
sólo el olvido es de la paz asilo.
Ni el hilo de la historia es hilo nuevo,
sino de sangre, la de Abel y Cristo,
con sangre la gallina se hace el huevo,
con huevo se hace sangre y... ¡todo listo!
Vanidad vino nuevo en viejo odre,
viejo en el nuevo vanidad lo mismo,
todo jugo de vida es sólo podre
y el zenit y el nadir un solo abismo.
Decir de nuevo lo que ya se dijo,
crear de nuevo la palabra muerta,
darle otra vuelta más al acertijo
y hacer con sombra y luz la muerte incierta.

47 **PHILOSOPHEMES**

The sayings of old in modern words recoined,
in every old day to see a new sun rise;
the line which starts from an immobile point,
like you, my soul, upon a point it dies.
With centuries you spin the thread of time,
in your hands the now becomes eternity;
the flowing sap in a present moment primes
the fruit to combat its fugacity.
All life is what comes next, a resurrection
of what has been yet wills to persevere;
the game of time is but sedimentation
within the abyss of the celestial sphere.
'What's new my friend?' one asks the humble seamster
patching old clothes. 'What's new? Not e'en the thread.'
History is tatters, shabby disaster
which we forget lest its path again we tread.
The thread of history is not new thread
but blood, blood that from Christ and Abel comes.
With its own blood the chicken makes its egg,
the egg will make its blood and all is done.
To pour new wine in old skins is vain action,
old wine in new skins likewise vanity;
the sap of life is only putrefaction,
zenith and nadir but one activity.
To say once more what was already said,
to give the riddle yet another twist,
to bring to life the word that has lain dead,
to paint in light and dark death lying in mist.

48 LA ÚLTIMA PALABRA DE HAMLET

The rest is silence
Hamlet, Act V, Sc ii

«El reposo es silencio», dijo Hamlet
a punto de morir, y sobre el suelo
su carne ensangrentada reclinando
    reanudó el silencio.

Y el ánimo, cual llama vacilante,
enraizado en el pábilo del cuerpo,
ondeaba invisible sacudido
    por contrapuestos vientos.

Le es silencio la muerte; el aire – entrañas
del mar celeste – duerme y sueña quedo,
las voces duermen, puede ser que sueñen,
    y se le para el pecho.

«¿Morir? Dormir..., dormir..., soñar acaso...»
y del reposo al fin en el silencio
– primer abrazo de la muerte virgen –
    arropose en el sueño.

«¡Ser o no ser!» Y para siempre Hamlet
quedose mudo, y mudo el universo
que le acogió con las tendidas alas
    en su callado seno.

¡Con los abiertos ojos ya sin vida,
como queriendo oír, miraba al cielo
– la mano de Dios la palma abierta –
    y caía el silencio!

48 HAMLET'S LAST WORD

The rest is silence
Hamlet, Act V, Sc ii

'The rest is silence,' Hamlet said
at point of death, and on the earth
his bloodied flesh he lay prostrate,
    and silence fell.

His soul, like a faltering flame
whose wick in the body lies afirm,
disturbed by gusts of fractious air
    quivered unseen.

For him, silence is death; the air,
remnant of the celestial sea,
abates and voices fade to dream;
    the heart desists.

'To die, to sleep, perchance to dream':
and wrapped in silence of an end
– the first embrace of virgin death –
    he took his rest.

'To be or not to be!' Hamlet
forever silent fell; the world
that received him in its bosom
    silent as well.

His open lifeless eyes were raised
to heaven – the open hand of God –
as if intent to hear His word;
    the silence held.

Una caída mansa; los instantes
goteaban sin rumor y en el sereno
– dulce llovizna en lago de una cumbre –
    se iban fundiendo.

Y el torturado espíritu del príncipe
íbase poco a poco derritiendo
en la mudez del ámbito que inmoble
    recogía su aliento.

«¡El reposo es silencio!» Reposaba
Hamlet, al cabo libre de secretos,
y a su pregunta eterna respondía
    el eterno silencio.

Gentle, soundless evanescence
as instants quietly drip – like rain
upon a mountain lake – to melt
    into the night.

To the muteness of the cosmos,
which motionless received his breath,
the tortured spirit of the Prince
    slowly recessed.

'The rest is silence!' And Hamlet
rested, free of all conspiracies,
and his eternal question met
    an endless still.

49 ANAMNESIS

En el campo de Dios, al aire libre,
bajo el cielo de todos,
junto al agua que al sol corre entre hierba,
nunca está el hombre solo.
En el seno desnudo de la tierra,
que al fin acoge a todos,
su atormentado corazón recuesta,
y ve morir el día
y nacer en el cielo las estrellas.

Y siente que se funde poco a poco
su atormentada vida
en la vida sin fin y sin principio
que en el cielo radica.

Pobre cordero, con los pies sangrientos
del mundo pedregoso,
el brazo allí del Rabadán divino
siente le ciñe en torno,
y sin saberlo él mismo se recuerda
de cuando allá en el cielo
era no más que una dormida idea
a la espera del cuerpo
en que vivir y amar a su albedrío
durante un breve ensueño.

49 REMINISCENCE

In God's unbounded fields, an open countryside
under a common sky,
next to the sunlit streams that through the meadows glide,
a man is not alone.
In the naked bosom of our earthly mother
who one day welcomes all,
he allows his weary body to recover
and sees the day decline
and the celestial stars their veil uncover.

He feels his life of torment then begin to blend,
as day fades into night,
into the life with no beginning and no end,
which in heaven resides.

Suffering lamb with feet that bleed from open wounds
caused by the stony soil,
he feels the clasp of that Great Shepherd from beyond
around his weary waist.
Unconsciously his memory recalls a time
when in a heavenly state
he was but an idea in a mind divine
waiting for the body
in which to live and gratify his will sublime
during a magic day.

CONCLUSION

50 [LA MUERTE ES SUEÑO]

Au fait, se disait-il à lui même, il parait
que mon destin est de mourir en rêvant.
Stendhal, *Le Rouge et le noir*

Morir soñando, sí, mas si se sueña
morir, la muerte es sueño; una ventana
hacia el vacío; no soñar; nirvana;
del tiempo al fin la eternidad se adueña.

Vivir el día de hoy bajo la enseña
del ayer deshaciéndose en mañana;
vivir encadenado a la desgana
¿es acaso vivir? ¿Y esto qué enseña?

¿Soñar la muerte no es matar el sueño?
¿Vivir el sueño no es matar la vida?
¿A qué al poner en ello tanto empeño:

aprender lo que al punto al fin se olvida
escudriñando el implacable ceño
–cielo desierto–del eterno Dueño?

50 DEATH IS A DREAM

Actually, he told himself, it would seem
that my fate is to perish in a dream.
Stendhal, *The Red and the Black*

To die while dreaming, yes, but if you dream
your death, death is a dream, an endless gaze
into the void; no dream; nirvanian haze
when eternity at last vanquishes time.

To live the present day within the reach
of yesterday as it becomes tomorrow;
to live manacled to chains of sorrow,
is that to live? What lesson does it teach?

To dream one's death, is that to kill a dream?
To live a dream, is that to kill one's life?
Why do we strive so eagerly to glean

what we can only fleetingly record
as we observe the unremitting mien
– an empty heaven – of the eternal Lord?

COMMENTARIES ON THE POEMS

1 RETURNING HOME
As Unamuno scholars we tend to forget that for the university rector, the political activist, the restless thinker, the most important part of his life was not to be found in any of these activities but in his family life. The mentions of his family in his correspondence leave little doubt: his heart lay in his home; and indeed his intense journalistic activities were undertaken in order to supplement his modest salary and provide for his large family. This beautiful poem brings out the contentment he found in his family and the way in which this helped to bolster his faith. The peaceful sleep of his children makes him think that they have entrusted their conscious life to a watchful Father for safe keeping while they rest.

2 HOME
This poem is a hymn of thanks to his wife Concha, who provided Unamuno with the solid, supportive home life which enabled him to shoulder his agitated public life and his inner spiritual restlessness. Her serene faith was a major factor in helping him to pull through during his crisis of depression in 1897. His *angina pectoris* (also mentioned in poem No. 6, but which did not, however, kill him until he was 72) made him meditate on death constantly, and in this poem he wonders what might have happened to him (death from cardiac disease, monastic seclusion, suicide) had he not enjoyed the tranquillity and enjoyment afforded by his home life. The full poem consists of six stanzas, of which the first two are reproduced here.

3 SWEET, SILENT THOUGHT
Most of Unamuno's writing was done not in solitude but at home surrounded by his family. This poem, which captures the contentment of his home life, paints a very different picture of Unamuno from that of the combative public figure which has come down to us. Though inspired in Shakespeare, this poem is not about the great Elizabethan poet but about Unamuno's own circumstances. The university professor of Greek, no doubt preparing his next lesson, sits at home on a winter's evening surrounded by his wife and children while he reads the renowned and entertaining classical historian Herodotus, whose approach to writing history was highly anecdotal and who mentions the riddles of the Oracle at Delphi. Lifting his eyes from the book, Unamuno looks into his wife's eyes and realizes that in them is all the wisdom that he needs. It is the experience of the family that provides him with the living knowledge that he seeks.

4 TO THE SICK CHILD

This is a lullaby dedicated to Raimundín, Unamuno's son, who early on developed hydrocephalus as a result of contracting meningitis and died at the age of seven. The poem was almost certainly written when the child was very ill and approaching death. It takes the form of traditional Spanish cradle songs, with the same rhythmic pattern, and captures in a simple, childlike way, the little boy's suffering and the father's heartbreaking attempt to console both the child and himself. This was an event that left a deep imprint on Unamuno and which he was to remember for the rest of his life, as other poems on the same topic attest. This one poem contains a subtle progression from the first to the last stanza, which harks back to the beginning but hints at the inevitable outcome.

5 UPON THE DEATH OF CONCHA

Concha Lizárraga played a crucial role in Unamuno's life. Not only did she bear him nine children, of whom eight survived into adulthood (Unamuno had always wanted a large family), but she became his sheet anchor amidst the tribulations brought on by his combative public stance in political, religious, and educational issues. In Concha Unamuno found a necessary refuge from the many stresses of his life. Her crystalline and trusting religious faith was an inspiration and a consolation for the doubt-ridden Unamuno. She died on 15 May 1934, two-and-a-half years before Unamuno himself. He wrote many poems devoted to her, both before and after her death. This one is a tribute to her memory, her warmth of character, and her unruffled disposition.

6 IN MY STUDY

This poem was written on New Year's eve, 1906, thirty years to the very day before Unamuno's death. Here he uses blank verse as he ponders his habit of meditating on death, of which his angina is a constant reminder. But it is a wholly personal, not an abstract or philosophical meditation. The poem suggests that what keeps him going is precisely his need to express his anxieties. Yet once again his family is there in the background as they assemble for dinner. The study of Unamuno's rectoral home (where this poem was written) can still be visited in the Casa-Museo Unamuno in Salamanca.

7 THE CHILD AND THE DOLL

Unamuno was a great observer of young children and, as is apparent from the poems he wrote about them, was often struck both by their questions and by their intuitively shrewd views of the world, as well as by the unconscious frankness with which they expressed themselves. Their innocent comments and desires often prompted Unamuno to reflect on the question of whether we retain primitive deep-seated ways of thinking about ourselves. A child's spontaneity was an indication of an in-built, non-rational appreciation of our world and our existence. In this poem the child, uninhibited by the presence of an adult, seems to display an instinctive awareness of the imagination as a powerful tool that confers on us the ability to expand beyond the world of our immediate experience.

8 CONCHA'S PRESENCE

Unamuno's marriage to Concha Lizárraga lasted forty-three years until her death in May 1934 after more than a month of almost total loss of physical and mental faculties. But as this poem shows, Unamuno continued to be deeply tied to her. The poem was written two short months after her death, a devastating loss for Unamuno, but one which inspired him to sublime poetic heights. In this poem he recognizes that Concha had been the mainstay of his life, that she had dedicated her whole married life to him, that her firm religious faith had more than made up for his shaky one, and that her entire outlook on life was based on love and not on the search for answers to irresolvable questions. The poem is of course a result of Concha's absence, but paradoxically Unamuno claims her presence: through her infinite capacity for love she has earned eternal peace, and that is why, says Unamuno, any complaint on his part would be inconsiderate. Though a celebration of Concha's constancy, the poem is also an eloquent expression of Unamuno's striving to combat the solitude of his widowerhood.

9 EMPTY SILENCE

Although it would be incorrect to say that Unamuno was a theologian, this poem is all the same a succinct guide to his wholly personal theology. Unamuno proposed that God and man are mutual creations. Man creates God to explain his provenance and final destiny. God creates man to earn recognition through our consciousness of Him. This follows from the biblical contention that God created man in his own image. Each person obtains confirmation of his or her own existence from the existence of others. Thus God needs us in the same way that we need Him. But what man really wants to know, argues Unamuno, is whether this creation is reality or illusion, and this, God does not tell us. Instead, driven by our 'blind' will to survive (as per Schopenhauer), we are obliged to rely on our reason to come up with arguments for His existence. But these arguments are spurious. God is not a rational phenomenon; He is an inexplicable yearning that we project outwards, and it is this inner yearning for transcendence that is our truth, the truth of God.

10 AFTER I CEASE TO BE

Throughout his adult life Unamuno experienced a mighty battle between belief and unbelief. He missed the simple faith of his childhood but knew he could never recover it. Instead he often described belief as a wanting to believe. For him belief meant above all the survival of his own consciousness, a continuing existence as himself and not simply a Pauline return to the Godhead. In this poem (of which the introductory verses have been omitted) Unamuno transfers his hope of personal survival to the survival of the very poem he is writing, and especially to the reader who on reading it will consider the poet's mortality as well as his own. He expresses his perplexity at the mystery of words, that they have the capacity to outlive and invoke the creator who lies beyond their reach. But his hope as he writes the poem is tempered by the thought that one day the song will follow the singer into oblivion. This is in consonance with Unamuno's belief that a universe without conscious observers is inconceivable. The world needs us as much as we need the world.

11 READING THE LIVING BOOK OF A DEAD FRIEND

This is one of Unamuno's most heartening poems on the theme of mortality. Unamuno's religious beliefs, which at times came close to pantheism despite his denials, required a communal God, a God whose existence was expressed through the community of his creatures. And conversely his creatures had God in common. Thus God saves us from an isolated and terminal individuality ('you from you and me from me', as the poem says). The death of one member does not destroy that commonality. So long as one of us is alive, all of us are alive. The presence of the dead is the presence of God.

12 WAITING

This poem takes the form of a ballad or *romance*, a poetic form that goes back to the Middle Ages and has always been popular. The story here is simple on the surface: an old woman is sitting outside the mill looking in the distance and obviously waiting for someone as night falls. We are not told who this person might be: her son, her husband expected back from delivering flour? The atmosphere becomes increasingly ominous and the reader cannot help thinking that it is Death that is on the way, symbolized by the spinning. The poem becomes more dreamlike as the woman and the windmill seem to change places in the fourth stanza, so that the mill now does the spinning and the woman the milling. The lane that leads away from the mill seems to stretch all the way up to the distant but beckoning stars.

13 RIVERS OF MY LIFE

In this poem Unamuno uses the rivers with which he became most familiar as metaphors of his life: an endless, agitated flow towards his origins. The Nervión is the river of his youth in Bilbao, the Tormes the river of his mature years in Salamanca, and the Bidasoa the river of his exile in Hendaye. Just as a river is impelled to return to its origins in the sea, so Unamuno sees his life as a restless journey which will take his soul to a peaceful conclusion or *desnacer* (an unbirth, as he called it), of which those quiet pools along the way are a prefigurement. The poem contains an obvious echo of the fifteenth-century poet Jorge Manrique's famous lines 'nuestras vidas son los ríos / que van a dar en la mar' ['our lives are the rivers / making their way to sea'].

14 RESTLESS HEART

This sonnet is a typically Unamunian cry of protest against finitude. He starts by invoking the Jesus of Teresa of Ávila. 'La más recóndita morada' is a reference to the *Tratado de las moradas* of St Teresa in which she describes the seven states or 'mansions' of the soul on the way to mystical union with Christ. But Unamuno plays with 'morar' (to dwell) and 'morir' (to die) in order to affirm the paradoxical right of humans to stake a claim for immortality on the basis of Christ's acceptance of mortality. The reward of eternal life is worth all suffering, as St Teresa consistently defended in her writings and as Unamuno not just recalls but demands. He repeatedly argued that for the gift of life, freely given, to be taken away would be a cruel irony, and contrary to a loving God as revealed by Jesus. But the uncertainty of our fate remains to trouble us.

15 THE ATHEIST'S PRAYER

Unamuno was anything but an orthodox believer. Indeed he was repeatedly denounced by the Spanish hierarchy as a heretic and many regarded him as an atheist. In fact he was no such thing. He simply held that religious or transcendental belief was not a matter of blindly accepting the Church's dogma. That was mere credulity. Real faith had to be fought for constantly; it was a creative striving. Atheists merely gave up the struggle, and in this respect were little different from the unquestioning mass of believers: neither made the effort to penetrate the mystery of our existence. In this poem he ironically portrays the atheist addressing his non-existent God. For Unamuno, a God whose existence we take for granted is as useless as a God whose non-existence we take for granted. Either way we are positing a truth that is beyond our reach. But beyond the irony of the poem one can sense a struggle to comprehend the notion of a divine being.

16 PSALM II

This poem is inspired by St Mark's account of the curing by Jesus of the young man who suffered from epilepsy, or 'dumb spirit' as it is called in the Gospel, following the father's famous appeal to Jesus 'Lord, I believe; help thou my unbelief' (St Mark, 9.24). But of course the poem is not about the Gospel incident but about Unamuno's personal way of believing. He takes a typically contradictory stance, insisting that God is unknowable, that faith is a mystery and death a reality required by faith, since eternal life, if achieved, would require no faith. To Unamuno's dialectical way of thinking, belief only becomes meaningful in the light of unbelief, which is why he was attracted to this particular passage from St Mark. The last seven verses of the poem are derived from St Mark, 9.17–24; and there are also biblical echoes in other verses. The poem is one of six psalms that appeared in Unamuno's first collection of poetry. It shows a wide metric variation, mixing pentasyllabic, heptasyllabic, octosyllabic and hendecasyllabic verses in no particular pattern, a poetic pragmatism that Unamuno was to abandon in later collections. Whilst retaining the metric variety of the original, the translation employs hexasyllabic, octosyllabic, and decasyllabic verses in groups of two to eight verses.

17 SALAMANCA

Unamuno retained his Basque allegiance throughout his life. Nevertheless his fondness for his adoptive town, its countryside, and its people became an intrinsic part of his legend. If Bilbao was his body, Salamanca was his soul. He arrived in the old Castilian town and its ancient university as Professor of Greek in 1891, just days after his 27th birthday, and died there in 1936 at the age of 72. Salamanca was to be the scene of his triumphs, struggles, and even frustrations, for he was not without local enemies. But he never wavered in his loyalty and devoted many poems to the city and its hinterland. The one included here is the most famous of all, and was set to music by the composer Joaquín Rodrigo in 1953. The beautiful golden stone of the old Salamancan buildings figures prominently in the poem.

18 LAND OF THE TORMES

Unamuno gave many talks in the Casa del Pueblo (rough equivalent of the WEA) situated in the street called Arco de la Lapa in Salamanca (changed in 2014 to Abogados de Atocha). In the afternoon, before retiring to his study, Unamuno was in the habit of taking exercise by walking to the outskirts of the city. The reference to the guide-boy and the blind man holds an allusion to the comic tale of 1554 *La vida de Lazarillo de Tormes*, but also and more immediately to his own walks with his blind friend and poet Cándido Rodríguez Pinilla. The Dominican convent of San Esteban, where Unamuno had many friends among the friars, was his first refuge upon the onset of his terrible crisis of March 1897, which plunged him into a deep depression. He spent three days there on that occasion.

19 TO THE RIVER TORMES

The River Tormes in Salamanca, crossed by an old Roman bridge, flows along the southern edge of the old city and forms a prominent feature of the landscape seen from the the top of the ramparts, as well as offering walks along its banks. This poem follows its course from the Gredos range, through the small towns of Guijo de Ávila and Santa Teresa, the larger town of Alba de Tormes and on to Salamanca. La Flecha was the countryside retreat of the Salamancan Augustinians and is mentioned by the sixteenth-century poet Fray Luis de León in his famous poem 'Qué descansada vida'. Juan Meléndez Valdés (1754–1817) is another poet who studied in Salamanca and worked there as lecturer and professor for eleven years, returning to live there in 1802. It is then that he wrote the bucolic poetry referred to by Unamuno in the final stanza.

20 THE ROCK OF FRANCE

The Sierra de la Peña de Francia, high up in the hills to the south of Salamanca, has a shrine to Our Lady of the same name which became a place of pilgrimage after the discovery of a statue in the fifteenth century. It was one of Unamuno's favourite places for excursions, especially after his friends, the Dominican friars, took over the running of the church and the convent in 1900. In this poem Unamuno imagines a connection between the BVM or historical mother of Jesus, the black statue of Our Lady of the Peña de Francia, and the remarkable Blanche of Castile, Queen Regent of France upon the death of her husband Louis VIII and whom Unamuno sees as the Rock of France. She was in fact the mother of two saints, since both her son King Louis IX and her daughter Isabelle were canonized. What the three women of the poem – two historical and one a mythical representation – have in common is their devotion and motherly solicitude. All three are revered as models of motherhood. For Unamuno, of course, the greatest model of motherhood was his own wife, whom he regarded not only as the biological mother of his children but also as his own spiritual mother. The crucial importance of the mother is a key and persistent theme in Unamuno's writing.

21 THE LAKE AT SAN MARTIN

In June 1930, a few months after his return from exile, Unamuno went to visit the Lago de Sanabria in the province of Zamora, just north of the Portuguese border. On the northern shore of the lake is the town of San Martín de Castañeda, one of several poor communities trying to scratch a living at the time of Unamuno's visit. It was the legend of a sunken village in the lake that inspired Unamuno to write his novel *San Manuel Bueno, mártir* (1931). In San Martín he also came across the ruins of a Cistercian monastery, which explains the reference to St Bernard. But the poem is primarily a meditation on the effects of time and on the ruinous condition and harsh living of the villages around the lake.

22 MEDINA DE RIOSECO

Medina de Rioseco, a historic town to the northwest of Valladolid, was a prosperous agricultural centre in the sixteenth and seventeenth centuries. A canal northwards from Medina, meant to reach the ports on the Cantabrian coast, was started in the middle of the eighteenth century but was never completed because the arrival of the railways made it uneconomic. On his visit to the town, Unamuno must have seen the abandoned and rotting barges on the banks of the canal (since then rehabilitated and open to river cruises). As is almost always the case, Unamuno contrasts past splendours with present decay. Past generations laboured hard to make the land productive, he says, but it still fails to meet the needs of today's inhabitants. The land is dominated by an unremittingly cloudless sky.

23 THE VOICE OF THE BELL

This somewhat unusual but striking poem is a tribute to the hardworking and impoverished peasants of western Spain in Extremadura and Old Castile. They are, says Unamuno, a hardened race who get on with their jobs on an unforgiving land without complaint or pleading. Their stoicism is like the peal of a bell that expresses its hope for a richer life without articulating a word. Only God can hear the tale of sorrow carried aloft by their silent song repeated through centuries of time. One interesting detail that we notice in this poem is that the angel is not sent by God to man, as is normally the case, but is rather sent by these simple yet devout people to God to carry their message to Him. For Unamuno, the direction of travel of divinity is from man to God.

24 PORTUGAL (i)

Unamuno was a devoted Lusophile, and often ventured into Portuguese territory from his relative isolation in Salamanca. He rated Portuguese literature of the nineteenth century far above Castilian literature and counted Antero de Quental, Eugenio de Castro, and Camilo Castelo Branco among his favourite authors. Not that he was starry-eyed about Portugal; he knew it was educationally backward and that tuberculosis was rife there. But this did not prevent Portuguese writers from capturing what Unamuno saw as the Iberian spirit, which modern (*i.e.* nineteenth-century) Castile had betrayed. The two poems dedicated to Portugal included here demonstrate Unamuno's formal diversity but thematic consistency. Despite their different forms, the two poems offer the same metaphorical texture.

25 PORTUGAL (ii)

Instead of the more varied metre of the preceding poem, this one uses hendecasyllables throughout in the more traditional sonnet form. But apart from the technical difference that gives this poem a more formal appearance and feel, the way Portugal is presented is almost identical: the woman on the seashore looking westwards out to sea, the pine-clad slopes above, the glorious and adventurous past of Portugal's seaborne empire, and above all the wistful memories of an indomitable spirit represented by the young, brave and reckless King Sebastian, and the legend of his return to lead his country once again.

26 MY OTHER FATE

Unamuno arrived in Fuerteventura on 10 March 1924 and spent exactly four months in exile on the island. He was approaching 60 when he left in July 1924. His stay on this barren, sparsely populated island gave him the opportunity to meditate on his agitated life, agitated both spiritually (because of his insistence on forging a Christianity more spiritual and less dogmatic, which brought him into conflict with the Catholic Church) and socially (because of his determination to denounce political authorities of a high-handed or militaristic disposition, which brought him into conflict with King Alfonso XIII and the Primo de Rivera regime). Although he continued to wage war unremittingly on Primo de Rivera, his stay in Fuerteventura brought out the more contemplative side of him. In this poem he ponders the person he might have been and the life he might have led had he not left Bilbao for a job in Salamanca, entirely as if one self has been exiled by the other. Unamuno regarded his potential but unfulfilled selves (he called them 'mis yos ex-futuros', my ex-future selves) as part of the problem of the determinism-versus-free will debate. What took him to Salamanca was pure chance, since he had been applying for posts all over Spain, including his native Bilbao; but in retrospect his life was indelibly marked by his association with his adoptive city and university.

27 DISTANT WAVES
During his stay in Fuerteventura Unamuno wrote poems about the island and its people, about the unhappy situation in Spain, about the wife he had had to leave behind, but above all he wrote poems about the sea. In a majority of the Fuerteventura poems the sea plays a role, and in some he addresses the sea directly. Brought up in Bilbao, Unamuno had been close to the sea, which of course was not the case in his adoptive city of Salamanca. His closeness to the sea in Fuerteventura brought back memories of his childhood. In the poem that precedes this one in the original collection he mentions his native city, 'que en las marinas sales de su ría recibe el don bendito de la mar libre' ['which through the salty waters of its estuary receives the free spirit of the sea']. In this poem he associates the sea with the rhythmic shanties he used to hear in Bilbao.

28 BETANCURIA
Betancuria, named after the conqueror of the island, Jean de Béthencourt, was the ancient capital of Fuerteventura and lies to the west of the island in a deep valley surrounded by barren hills. The poem recounts Unamuno's visit to the village, which he describes exactly as he found it in June 1924: whitewashed houses with geraniums outside forming a poor, isolated settlement, *majoreras* in native costume at prayer in the church, and on the mountain above the figure of a camel bending down to look for some trace of vegetation on the stony ground. What Unamuno adds is his admiring reflexion on the stoicism and unflagging faith of those impoverished inhabitants.

29 FUERTEVENTURA
In Fuerteventura Unamuno discovered an island uncontaminated by the pressures and petty squabbles of a modern civilization. His stay on the island left him deeply impressed, above all by the warmth and fortitude of the local inhabitants who, despite grinding poverty, retained a cheerful, uncomplaining outlook. This played a major part in Unamuno's own recovery after the hurt and ignominy of the brutal removal from his university post and distant exile away from the scene of his protests against authoritarian politics. After a stay of four months he left what was then a remote place

to settle in France in order to be nearer to his family, and despite not fulfilling his wish to return to the island, the experience of Fuerteventura was one he was never to forget. This sonnet is Unamuno's expression of gratitude, and proclaims that his mysterious faith was restored by the calming effect of this barren environment. The real desert, paradoxically, is to be found in the midst of civilization, not in the parched lands of Fuerteventura. This was his farewell poem to the island, written on board ship shortly after setting sail for France from Las Palmas.

30 IN EXILE
Despite an amnesty which allowed his return to Spain, Unamuno refused to return so long as the man who exiled him so arbitrarily, the dictator General Miguel Primo de Rivera, remained in power. After four months in Fuerteventura, he left on 9 July 1924 first for Las Palmas and then for Paris, where he lived for a year, and thence to Hendaye, where he could be reached more easily by his family, and where he was to remain for four-and-half years (until the fall of Primo de Rivera early in 1930), returning in triumph to Salamanca on 13 February 1930. For Unamuno, Hendaye and the surrounding French hills and river Bidasoa were part of his native Basque country, and he settled there to a relatively peaceful existence of reading and writing. Poetically, this was a productive period, and most of the *Cancionero*, which amounts to about half of Unamuno's poetic production, was composed during these years. From Hendaye, Unamuno liked to glance across the mouth of the river Bidasoa and the town of Fuenterrabía to mount Jaizkibel on the Spanish side.

31 FRONTIER BALLADS
The shifting frontier played a crucial role in Spanish medieval history, defining the fortunes of Christians for many centuries while they attempted to regain, during the *reconquista,* the land lost to the Muslims in the invasion of 711. Many towns in southern Spain still bear the additament 'de la frontera' after their name. The military campaigns and clashes between Christians and Moors (as they were called) gave rise to many ballads or *romances*. Unamuno considers his own exile from Spain as a war of reconquest which he has to wage against those who have taken over Spain, and he expresses the hope that his songs of defiance will earn him his fame. Altobiscar is a mountain in the western Pyrenees on the frontier between France and Spain just above Roncesvaux, where the troops of Charlemagne were defeated by Basques in 778. The Canto de Altobiscar celebrating this victory is a Basque hymn full of nationalist sentiment, but its ancient pedigree is in dispute.

32 REMEMBER US
In the church at Biriatou, a village in the French Pyrenees near Hendaye, Unamuno came across a memorial stone bearing the names of eleven local men who died in the Great War. Underneath their names was the inscription, in Basque, 'Orhoit gutaz', remember us. Unamuno took down the names of all eleven sons of Biriatou (which

he reproduced in the original version) and dedicated this poem to their memory. But the poem is not just a poignant memorial but also a powerful protest against the senselessness of a war that deprived mothers of their sons to no meaningful purpose. Beneath the peaceful atmosphere of the bucolic scene there is the sense of regret, the terrible 'why?' question that one no-one wants to face as we choose to go about our daily business.

33 THE CEMETERY AT HENDAYE
A visit to the cemetery at Hendaye leads Unamuno to one of his frequent meditations on mortality. Here the tone is of resignation tinged with sadness at the absence of the dead, who nevertheless remain spiritually present in our consciousness. As is very often the case in Unamuno the surrounding landscape has a part to play – the river Bidasoa as it flows into the Bay of Biscay, the sea-breeze, the sun, the moon, the tide, the houses that surround the cemetery – but the underlying subject of the poem is the fleetingness of human life compared to the ceaseless flow of time. Everything reminded Unamuno of finitude. The broken fourth verse of every stanza has the jarring effect of making us pull up short and refocus.

34 THE FACES OF POETRY
Unamuno often mixes in a single poem several of his enduring preoccupations: the impossibility of arriving at a transcendent truth, the unreliability of language, the puzzling existential freedom of the human being, and the value of each one of us as a centre of consciousness without which the universe would not exist. Only a mystical sense of existence can overcome the contradictions of the human condition, but poetry comes closest to revealing the truth about ourselves because it obeys a deep creative impulse and not simply the discursive dimension of our brain. Poetic creativity appears to have no limits, comes to no conclusions; it covers both 'yes' and 'no'. The harmony of a poem does not depend on the logical consistency of reason. It relies rather for its effect on what Unamuno calls 'canción', melody or song, its ability, that is, to transport us to another sphere.

35 THE TASK OF THE POET
This poem is built around one of Unamuno's most persistent ideas, that of the intimate connection, even equivalence, of language and thought. Do we have language in order to express our thoughts? Or are our thoughts the result of having language? Does the poet have something to say prior to the poem's existence? Or does he discover the substance of the poem only as he composes it? Unamuno uses St Thomas Aquinas's idea of the incompleteness of the disembodied (or inert) soul and the disensouled (or inanimate) body. Each needs the other to express itself. To this Unamuno adds the poet's complaint that there is no answer to his question of whether the poem belongs to him or to language; but the 'ars longa, vita brevis' sentiment of the closing lines has a hint of the religious about it: we can only hope to endure creatively whilst acknowledging

our transience. The poem uses simple, unobtrusive assonance in the even verses; the assonance is a little more obvious in the final stanza. The translation uses blank verse throughout bar the final stanza, which has an element of rhyme and assonance.

36 THE VIBRANT WORD

Writing was for Unamuno a form of self-discovery. He learnt about himself as he wrote, even though he also admitted that when he re-visited works of his the personality he discerned in them seemed alien to him. This simple poem expresses the idea of writing as an expression of the self. It is not only a matter of forging iron as a blacksmith does, but equally of communicating creatively through the living power of words. Unamuno held an expressive – as distinct from representational – theory of language, while conceding that language was refractory and exceedingly difficult to tame.

37 THE CRUEL WORD

The simplicity of this poem is deceptive. The inversion of subject and predicate at the end of the first stanza and the hyperbaton in the second (normal syntax would give 'y la palabra, al abrigo de fe, me da mi trastrigo') obscures the sense on a first reading. But what Unamuno is saying is that anyone who dabbles in words will get his comeuppance because language will always have the last word. Which only goes to show that Derrida had been well antedated by Unamuno and Mauthner, both of whom argued for the autonomy of language.

38 THE WORD AS SYMBOL

This poem proposes a theory of language that verges on the sacred. Unamuno defended the close connection between language and thought, going sometimes as far as to identify the two ('pensamos con palabras' – 'we think with words'). Language was in particular what enabled us to imagine worlds that go beyond our material circumstances, in effect to move in symbolic, as distinct from purely physical, realms. Linguistic symbols, then, add immeasurably to our experience. From this perspective, language appears almost as a world of its own that goes beyond its phonetic reality and points to a transphysical dimension of existence. Here Unamuno has in mind the biblical phrase 'In the beginning was the Word' (St John, 1.1). Like the nineteenth-century Oxford-based German linguistician Max Müller (whose writings he knew), Unamuno held that religion was largely a linguistic construct, and that theology was really theography. For him, one of the greatest poets was Jesus of Nazareth, precisely because of the beauty and appeal of his metaphors and parables.

39 NOT ALL OF ME WILL DIE

The Roman poet Horace claimed that in his poetry he had built a monument for posterity which would ensure his immortality. There was very probably a touch of irony in this, but Unamuno assumes that Horace was speaking seriously and takes him to task for equating posthumous fame with immortality. This of course suggests that Unamuno did not think such survival in art was in any way comparable to survival in the flesh, that is, the survival of individual consciousness. This is indeed stated by Unamuno in several other places in his work, and the proposition frequently encountered in Unamuno criticism that his creative urge was led by his ambition to survive and thereby cheat death must be heavily nuanced to carry conviction. The works may indeed survive and convey a strong impression of the artist, but that of course is an impression wholly dependent on others as observers; it has nothing to do with the survival of the artist *qua* individual. Horace, says Unamuno, craftily challenges others to forget him, but he in turn forgot that those others will pass just as he himself has passed, and then his work will be worthless. The idea behind this poem is very close to that expressed in the closing lines of poem No. 10.

40 THE NAME OF MAN
The Book of Genesis tells us that as God created he named. And having created Adam, he invited him to follow his example and name all living creatures. From this Unamuno took his cue and said that 'nombrar es crear', to name is a creative act; but a creative act that needs an I and a You, an originator and a receptor. For Unamuno, the creative power of language pointed to a transcendent being. Language only makes sense when there is a You as well as an I. The mutuality between God and man is achieved through the creative power of naming.

41 THE CHILDREN OF SILENCE
Technically this may not be one of Unamuno's better poems but it does reveal something about his intimate preferences. The poem expresses a deep disappointment about the lack of acceptance on the part of the public of his 'sons of silence'. Whereas his adoptive children, those without pedigree taken from the orphanage, make a splash, his natural sons are ignored. Unamuno said on more than one occasion that his ideas were not new; he was simply recycling them in refurbished garb. It is his personal vision, his deepest sentiments, that Unamuno valued; but it is his outbursts against Church, State and conventional thinking that gave him fame. It is not hard to guess that those authentic children of his are precisely his poems, which did not gain him recognition as a poet. The idea of an author as a father, in parallel with that of God as creator, is central to Unamuno's aesthetic theory.

42 KANT AND THE FROG
In this ingenious poem Unamuno compares the natural world with the world of abstract concepts. When as dusk falls the poet shuts his book (Kant's *Critique of Pure Reason*, to judge by the reference to noumena), he feels himself communing with nature and recognizes the solidity of the natural world as against the artificiality of a man-made world made of empty words. It is the frog searching for a mate that strikes the note of authenticity. The reference to Kant in the last verse is somewhat ambiguous. Does the

poet admire Kant because he had the temerity to construct a complex theory of human knowledge (that the world conforms to our mind and not our mind to the world) thereby placing man above nature, or because he placed strict limits on such knowledge? It is more likely that, despite his scepticism ('the massive lie'), what he admires is Kant's creativity in going beyond what we observe.

43 ARE WE FREE?

The long-standing determinism-versus-free will debate was one that Unamuno found arid, as he made clear in several of his essays. For him the debate is irresolvable, because although we certainly feel free when we think about our future and we take action accordingly, there is no guarantee that our past has not been in some way determined. The river appears to carve its own course on its way to the sea, but did it have any alternative?

44 GOD AND THE WORD

In the Book of Exodus, 33.20, we read: 'And he said, Thou canst not see my face: for no man shall see my face and live.' Why did God refuse to show Moses his face, yet ordered him to convey his words to the Jews? Unamuno picks upon the paradox that we know of God only through texts or words. The power of words is greater than the power of objects, he suggests. He could of course have argued by analogy that staring at the sun will destroy our eyesight, but instead he argues that our expectations or hope of survival cannot be based on what we observe around us, since we do not see any such survival, and must therefore be based on an inner voice, on our creative imagination which we express through words, on something certainly invisible but not thereby unreal, since after all we are surrounded by invisible realities. Our past, too, is largely recorded in words ('a store of recitations'). There may be (more particularly in the third stanza) an implied reference to Kantian philosophy, whose 'words' have paradoxically had a greater impact (at least in the philosophical world) than the world of phenomena, that is of appearances. In any case the poem is typically Unamunian in that a passing detail picked up on a chance reading straightaway alerts his mind to all kind of inferences and ramifications, in this case the close connection between language and spirituality.

45 ENTROPY

Entropy, or the tendency towards thermodynamic equilibrium, brings about the utter stillness or death of a system in which there is no heat to exchange and thereby cause activity. Unamuno uses the concept to offer a brief meditation on the mystery of time. It inevitably reminds us today of the physicists' account of time slowing down as the space ship approaches a black hole and then appears to be frozen in time on the edge of it. Though using the concept of a frozen universe, Unamuno is not of course thinking of space travel; he is thinking of the impossibility of reconciling our time-bound vision of the universe with the Creator's own timelessness. At what point do they meet?

46 THE HANDS OF THE CLOCK

This simple poem is derived from Thomist philosophy, to which Unamuno appears to have subscribed. A human person is composed of body and soul, and each needs the other to find fulfilment and expression. The clock has a mechanism that can work without the hour and minute hands, but it then becomes a pointless contraption that has no reason for existing. The biological mechanism that is man has likewise no *raison d'être*; if we cannot think and choose we are mere automatons without significance. What interested Unamuno was of course the origins and implications of our freedom. Do our bodies give our soul or being its freedom, or viceversa? One would have expected the penultimate verse to read 'en un cuerpo desalmado' ['in a body without spirit'], meaning that we need our souls to give us our sense of freedom, but in fact what Unamuno seems to be saying is that the loss of our body at death deprives our spirit of the freedom of choice we enjoy while alive.

47 PHILOSOPHEMES

Unamuno liked to quote the biblical maxim *nihil novum sub sole* (Book of Ecclesiastes). He declared that his own ideas were not new but rather recycled; what he endeavoured to do was to give them new expression, or style as he called it. As a professor of classics he was well aware that many of the ideas that we take as modern are nothing of the kind and can be found in Greek and Roman writers. In this poem he meditates on life as endless repetition: we are part of the life-death cycle, momentary scintillations of conscious will amidst the blind, unconscious will or energy of the cosmos. Schopenhauerian through and through (Schopenhauer was the philosopher who left the biggest imprint on Unamuno), this poem is wistfully pessimistic, its rich abab rhyme pattern emphasizing the theme of recurrence. The 'acertijo' or riddle (of life, in this case) contains an oblique reference to the enigmatic prophecies of the Pythia or Oracle at Delphi, pronouncements which had to be interpreted by the priests. The reference to 'new wine in old skins' comes from the Gospel of St Mark, 2.22: 'No man putteth new wine into old bottles.'

48 HAMLET'S LAST WORD

Shakespeare was one of Unamuno's favourite authors, not least because of the English playwright's extraordinary ability to express sentiments in a striking and memorable manner. That is what Unamuno admired most in great writers: the uniqueness of style, the ability to express ordinary things in fresh ways. In this poem Unamuno himself turns the Christian idea of virgin birth into the paradoxical virgin death which leads us to a different mode of existence. He also appears to misinterpret Hamlet's dying words, 'the rest is silence', but we cannot be certain whether he does so deliberately or unknowingly, or indeed whether the ambiguity belongs to Shakespeare in the first place. Unamuno interprets Hamlet's death pantheistically, not as destruction but rather as a passing into universal unconsciousness, represented by the silence which is repeatedly invoked in the poem. The image of raindrops disappearing into the dark, mysterious waters of the mountain lake is one that Unamuno used to great poetic effect in *San Manuel Bueno, mártir*, where the raindrops transmute into snowflakes falling on the lake of Valverde de Lucerna. In Schopenhauerian terms, we are temporary condensations of energy which return to the vast sea of the universe whence we came.

49 REMINISCENCE

This poem was written in the village of Matilla de los Caños del Río during one of Unamuno's many excursions to the countryside around Salamanca. It is a meditation inspired by the surrounding land and river. As in poem No. 23, Unamuno brings in the condition of the peasantry and the harshness of their lives, but this undoubted reality serves to underpin the intense desire for transcendence, for a spiritual life beyond the gruelling toil of a material existence under the challenging conditions of the extreme climate and the difficult lands of the Castilian plateau. The existence of the Great Shepherd in the sky reminds these Unamunian countryfolk that it was He who sent them out to look after his flocks and that to Him they will one day return. The theme of the poem is the Platonic doctrine of the soul's origin in the world of Ideas, of which we have but a faint reminiscence during our brief embodiment in the material world in which we find ourselves. As often in Unamuno, the question of the purpose of our corporeal lives and our fleeting freedom is one that will not go away. The 'para qué' ['what for'] question dominated his thought.

50 DEATH IS A DREAM

This poem was written just three days before Unamuno's death on the last day of 1936. It very clearly demonstrates his undiminished faculties, as he uses his favourite form, the sonnet, to express a sombre mood of helplessness. The poem reflects Unamuno's terrible circumstances in his final days. Confined to his house by the military authorities after a very public confrontation two-and-half months earlier with General Millán Astray, one of Franco's most brutal henchmen, now virtually alone and a figure of suspicion in a Salamanca that had become Nationalist, he is fully aware that his beloved country is tearing itself apart in a murderous frenzy. The poem exudes pessimism, even frustration in the unanswered questions which it asks. Nirvana was not a positive state of being for Unamuno. In a poem written two years earlier he had said that nirvana meant 'desgana', a lack of appetite or interest, in other words a wish to forget life. Unamuno was subject to depressive states, and this poem captures just such a state obliquely but eloquently. Yet there still persists the Romantic element of protest against an incomprehensible, and therefore unjust, fate. 'La muerte es sueño' ['Death is a dream'] is an inversion of Calderón's famous 'La vida es sueño' ['Life is a dream']. It is a fitting end to Unamuno's long and productive literary career in which he struggled incessantly to come to terms with the question mark against human existence but did so in the context of a living literary tradition.

Printed and bound by CPI Group (UK) Ltd, Croydon, CR0 4YY

13/04/2025

14656593-0003